QUILTING AT THE COTTAGE

"Your Inspiration Destination"

by Pearl Louise Krush

QUILTING AT THE VILLAGE

Published by

All American Crafts, Inc.
7 Waterloo Road
Stanhope, NJ 07874
www.allamericancrafts.com

Publisher | **Jerry Cohen**

Chief Executive Officer | **Darren Cohen**

Product Development Director | **Brett Cohen**

Editor | **Sue Harvey**

Art Director | **Kelly Albertson**

Technical Illustrator | **Rory Byra**

Photography | **Kevin Eilbeck**
KE Photography

Product Development
Manager | **Pamela Mostek**

Vice President/Quilting Advertising
& Marketing | **Carol Newman**

Every effort has been made to ensure that the information presented is accurate. Since we have no control over physical conditions, individual skills, or chosen tools and products, the publisher disclaims any liability for injuries, losses, untoward results, or any other damages which may result from the use of the information in this book. Thoroughly read the instructions for all products used to complete the projects in this book, paying particular attention to all cautions and warnings shown for that product to ensure their proper and safe use.

Printed in China
©2010 All American Crafts, Inc
ISBN:978-0-9819762-4-2
Library of Congress
Control Number: 2010936551

Dedication

I would like to dedicate this book to the many men and women who have inspired me. To my creative mother and both of my grandmothers who taught me many lessons during my childhood and to all of the women who have supported me during my creative career.

To my wonderful staff who are always here to support me. We have shared tons of work and oodles of adventures through the years. I am sure that without them many of my ideas and designs would not have come to fruition. Thank you to Julie Weaver, Cindy Reil, Cathy Teeslink, Marilyn Denison, Marie Craig, Brenda Less, Kimber Hoops and Jessica Teeslink. A special thanks to the talented Vickie Barlean for her machine quilting of the large projects in this book. In the future I'm sure we will all move on to another life adventure, but you will still be a part of Pearl Louise Designs.

Thanks also to my darling husband, Fred, who has always supported me with his kind and loving attention.

Contents

The Thimble Cottage Quilt Village

1960s. Next door to the hotel was a lovely Victorian home built in 1914.

In the early 1970s, the two buildings were connected with a large foyer and entrances added on both the front and back center of the very large building. It was called Ginny's Village and 12 different businesses were housed inside. The businesses included a jewelry shop, a dress shop, a gift shop, several beauty shops, a tobacco shop, a real-estate office, an Italian restaurant and an English teashop.

At this time I had opened my quilt shop across the alley from Ginny's Village. I can remember looking out my office window and dreaming about hanging quilts on the banister.

A variety of businesses came and went over the years, and then a bookstore, Internet café and sandwich shop opened, taking up all of the rooms. During this time I had moved my shop to a darling small two-story house located on Mt. Rushmore Road just a few blocks away.

I was surrounded by family as a child. My great-grandfather lived behind us in a small house, and he always had a special project he was working on. He would often include my siblings and me when building his projects. One summer he built us a playhouse using 2x2's stacked liked logs. Each row of wood was nailed together until the small 8' x 8' structure (complete with working windows, door and a covered porch) was completed. While building the playhouse, I learned a great deal about pulling, straightening and pounding nails. These lessons would be needed as I grew older and moved my business from one building to another. One very important memory about that time still stays with me: the playhouse was the place where I invented one business after another. At the age of eleven, I had become an entrepreneur and would continue being one for the rest of my life.

The playhouse I now play in is the Thimble Cottage Quilt Village. The building in which the business resides is full of history and has many storiesto tell. One side of the building was originally a doctor's residence built in 1934. This section of the building became the Dinosaur Hotel during the

One day while driving down the street, I saw that the bookstore was closing. I called the owner of the building and asked if I could have a key so that I could look at the building. The minute I entered I knew that I wanted to move the Thimble Cottage Quilt Shop into the very

large and very dark building. Over the next few weeks my staff and I removed over 60 walnut-stained bookshelves plus numerous bookcases and display cases. We then cleaned and moved our inventory and display pieces in. I knew my dream was coming true.

Today, each room, nook and cranny is filled with wonderful fabrics, notions, patterns, books and gifts for all of our visitors to enjoy. The design room is always filled with new projects being designed for classes or patterns for the Pearl Louise Designs pattern company housed in the same space. New collections of fabrics are designed and painted in the kitchen area of the shop.

Millions of tourists visit our area every year to enjoy attractions such as Mt. Rushmore, the Crazy Horse Monument, and Custer State Park. The Thimble Cottage Quilt Village has become a popular stop for many of them as they tour these attractions amid the beautiful Black Hills of South Dakota.

I simply love this business of creating, producing and entertaining. The fabrics, patterns and designs are never ending. I realize that growth in this industry is both in shops and online. I'm a little hesitant, but at the same time very excited, about building an online business. I do know it is the way of the future and so

very convenient for those who can't visit the shop in person. I invite you to visit The Thimble Cottage Quilt Village website, www.thimblecottage.com. There you will find all of our products, newsletters and the Guildy Girls Friendship Club.

As you turn the pages of this book, imagine walking through each and every room taking in all of the displays and the comforts of a cozy, warm, and wonderful quilt shop. Come enjoy The Thimble Cottage Quilt Village, home of Pearl Louise Designs, "Your Inspiration Destination."

As always, thank you for visiting,
Pearl Louise

Chapter 1

Four Seasons Foyer

When my new line of Petal Pushers fabrics arrived at the shop I knew it would be the star attraction of the foyer. Spring and summer prints are always so inviting and this one almost sparkles with freshness. I can see the quilt thrown over a hammock in the backyard or on a porch swing. Of course a pitcher filled with lemonade, a tray of cookies and a good book would be part of the day. What a great way for any girl to have some time out and be surrounded by the glorious colors and prints of summer.

As you look around the foyer, you will see many projects created with this fabric line. The Petal Pusher Block of the Month hangs behind the counter and shares the space with the panel wall quilt. The stairwell is filled with the Petal Pusher free pattern provided by Troy-Corp. The table is covered with a fun set of Star Flower Placemats and Potholders. If you want to be ever-so-stylish be sure to check out the new Bubblicious Bag and the Chic Shopper Tote. All of these items are so fun and so functional!

Daisy Days Quilt & Pillow

This charming quilt would be stunning made with any print or fabric.
The on-point setting adds a touch of style and the border technique frames the
quilt with a unique design. The center panel is repeated in a decorative accent pillow.

Skill Level: Beginner
Finished quilt size: 80" x 96"
Finished pillow size: 21" x 21"
Block size sewn into quilt: 9" x 9"
Number of blocks: 18

SUPPLIES

Yardage is based on 42"-wide cotton fabric.
- 3/4 yard white print
- 3/4 yard muslin
- 7/8 yard green basket-weave print
- 1 1/2 yards red polka-dot floral
- 1 7/8 yards yellow daisy print
- 2 1/4 yards red/white polka dot
- 2 1/3 yards yellow basket-weave print
- 3 3/8 yards light blue floral
- 88" x 104" piece of backing fabric
- 88" x 104" piece of batting
- 24" x 24" piece of batting
- Thread in colors to match fabrics
- 1 yard fusible web
- 20" pillow form
- Rotary cutter, ruler and mat
- Basic sewing supplies

CUTTING INSTRUCTIONS

From the white print, cut:
One 18 1/2" x 42" strip: recut into two 18 1/2" squares
Two 1 1/2" x 42" strips; recut into forty-four 1 1/2" squares

From the muslin, cut:
One 24" x 42" strips; recut into one 24" square (pillow lining)

From the green basket-weave print, cut:
Four 3 7/8" x 42" strips; recut into thirty-six 3 7/8" squares
Appliqué pieces as per instructions

From the red polka-dot floral, cut:
Two 21 1/2" x 28" rectangles (pillow backing)
Appliqué pieces as per instructions

From the yellow daisy print, cut:
Three 9 1/2" x 42" strips; recut into ten 9 1/2" squares
Two 15 1/2" x 42" strips; recut into four 15 1/2" squares and two 8 3/4" squares. Cut the 15 1/2" squares twice diagonally to make fourteen setting triangles. Cut the 8 3/4" squares in half once diagonally to make four corner triangles.

From the red/white polka dot, cut:
Twenty-one 1 1/2" x 42" strips; recut into sixty-eight 1 1/2" x 9 1/2" strips, six 1 1/2" x 19 1/2" strips and two 1 1/2" x 21 1/2" strips
Seven 1 1/2" x 42" strips (border)
Twelve 2 1/2" x 42" strips (binding)
Appliqué pieces as per instructions

From the yellow basket-weave print, cut:
Four 1" x 42" strips; recut into four 1" x 18 1/2" strips and four 1" x 19 1/2" strips
Two 3 1/2" x 42" strips; recut into eighteen 3 1/2" squares
Four 2 1/2" x 42" strips (border)
Four 3 1/2" x 42" strips (border)
Nine 4 1/2" x 42" strips; recut into thirty-six 4 1/2" x 8 1/2" rectangles
Appliqué pieces as per instructions

From the light blue floral, cut:
Six 3 1/2" x 42" strips; recut into seventy-two 3 1/2" squares
Four 3 7/8" x 42" strips; recut into thirty-six 3 7/8" squares
Nine 4 1/2" x 42" strips; recut into thirty-six 4 1/2" x 8 1/2" rectangles and four 4 1/2" squares
Nine 4 1/2" x 42" strips (border)

INSTRUCTIONS

Note: Use a 1/4" seam allowance throughout. Sew all pieces with right sides together and raw edges aligned. Press seams toward the darker fabric after adding each piece or as indicated.

Flower Panels
Note: Refer to the basic instructions for Fusible Appliqué on page 92 to prepare flower squares.
   1. Prepare fusible appliqué pieces for the petals, stems, leaves and flower centers using the patterns given in the pull-out pattern section.

Tip: Apply lightweight fusible interfacing to the wrong side of light-color fabrics to prevent shadowing when they are fused on top of darker fabrics.

   2. Fuse and stitch one flower motif on each 18 1/2" white print square. Set aside one flower square for the pillow.
   3. Sew a 1" x 18 1/2" yellow basket-weave strip to two opposite sides of the remaining flower square.

4. Sew the 1" x 19½" yellow basket-weave strips to the remaining sides of the flower square.

5. Sew a 1½" x 19½" red/white polka-dot strip to two opposite sides of the flower square.

6. Sew a 1½" white print square to the ends of two 1½" x 19½" red/white polka-dot strips.

7. Sew the pieced strips to the remaining sides of the flower square to complete the 21½" x 21½" flower panel.

Nine-Patch Blocks

1. Draw a diagonal line on the wrong side of the 3⅞" light blue floral squares.

2. Place a marked square right sides together with a 3⅞" green basket-weave square. Sew ¼" on each side of the drawn line. Cut apart on the drawn line. Open and press to complete two corner units. Repeat to make 72 corner units total.

¼"   **Make 72**

3. Sew a 3½" light blue floral square to two opposite sides of a 3½" yellow basket-weave square to make the block center row. Press seams toward the light blue squares. Repeat to make 18 center rows total.

Make 18

4. Sew a corner unit to two opposite sides of the remaining 3½" light blue floral squares to make 36 block side rows. Press seams toward the light blue floral squares.

Make 36

5. Sew a center row between two side rows to complete one 9½" x 9½" block. Press seams toward the center row. Repeat to make 18 blocks total.

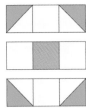

Make 18

Scallop Border Units

1. Fold each 4½" x 8½" yellow basket-weave rectangle in half with wrong sides together and lightly crease. Unfold.

2. Place a creased rectangle right side down on your ironing surface. Fold the bottom corners to meet the creased centerline at the top edge of the rectangle. Press.

3. Place the folded piece right side up and turn the pressed folded edges up to form curves. The curves should be ½" at the center and narrow to a point at the corners. Press and pin to hold the curves in place.

½"

4. Place the folded and pressed piece on the right side of a 4½" x 8½" light blue floral rectangle. Stitch the top edges of the two pieces together using a scant ⅛" seam allowance. Carefully topstitch the curved edges in place to complete one scallop unit.

5. Repeat steps 2–4 to make 36 scallop units total.

QUILT ASSEMBLY AND FINISHING

Note: Refer to the Assembly Diagram throughout the following steps. Press seams toward each border strip as added.

Assembly Diagram

1. Sew three Nine-Patch blocks together with two $9\frac{1}{2}$" yellow daisy print squares, thirteen $1\frac{1}{2}$" x $9\frac{1}{2}$" red/white polka-dot strips, eight $1\frac{1}{2}$" white print squares and one yellow daisy print setting triangle to make a center block section. Press seams toward the red/white polka-dot strips. Repeat to make a second center block section. Sew the center block sections to two opposite sides of the flower panel to complete the diagonal center section. Press seams toward the flower panel.

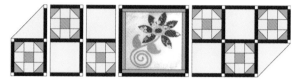

2. Sew the remaining Nine-Patch blocks, yellow daisy print squares, and red/white polka-dot strips together to make block rows. Press seams toward the polka-dot strips. Sew red/white polka-dot strips and white print squares together to make sashing rows. Press seams toward the polka-dot strips. Sew a sashing row to each block row. Press seams toward the sashing rows. Add a yellow daisy print setting triangle to each end of the pieced rows. Press seams toward the polka-dot strips. Join the pieced rows to make a diagonal corner section. Press seams toward the sashing rows. Repeat to make a second diagonal corner section.

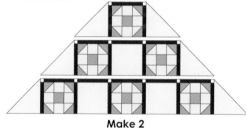

Make 2

3. Sew a corner section to opposite sides of the center section and sew a yellow daisy print corner triangle to each corner to complete the $58\frac{1}{2}$" x $72\frac{1}{2}$" quilt center. Press all seams toward the sashing rows.

4. *Red Border.* Sew the $1\frac{1}{2}$" x 42" red/white polka-dot strips short ends together to make a long strip. Cut two $72\frac{1}{2}$" lengths and two $60\frac{1}{2}$" lengths. Sew the longer strips to the sides and the shorter strips to the top and bottom of the quilt center.

5. *Yellow Border.* Sew the $2\frac{1}{2}$" x 42" yellow basket-weave strips short ends together to make a long strip. Cut two $74\frac{1}{2}$" lengths. Sew a strip to the sides of the quilt center. Sew the $3\frac{1}{2}$" x 42" yellow basket-weave strips short ends together and cut two $64\frac{1}{2}$" lengths. Sew a strip to the top and bottom.

6. *Scallop Border.* Sew 10 scallop units short ends together to make a side strip. Press seams in one direction. Repeat to make a second side strip. Sew the strips to the sides of the quilt. Press seams back toward the yellow border. Sew

eight scallop units short ends together to make the top strip. Repeat to make the bottom strip. Sew these strips to the top and bottom of the quilt. Press seams back toward the yellow border.

7. *Floral Border.* Sew the $4\frac{1}{2}$" x 42" light blue floral strips short ends together to make a long strip. Cut two $88\frac{1}{2}$" lengths and two $80\frac{1}{2}$" lengths. Sew the longer strips to the sides and the shorter strips to the top and bottom of the quilt center.

8. Layer, quilt and bind the quilt using the twelve $2\frac{1}{2}$" x 42" red/white polka-dot binding strips, referring to the Finishing Basics on page 92. Set aside remaining binding for the pillow.

PILLOW ASSEMBLY AND FINISHING

1. Sew a $1\frac{1}{2}$" x $18\frac{1}{2}$" yellow basket-weave print to two opposite sides of the remaining flower square and a $1\frac{1}{2}$" x $19\frac{1}{2}$" yellow basket-weave print to the remaining sides. Press seams toward the strips.

2. Sew a $1\frac{1}{2}$" x $19\frac{1}{2}$" red/white polka-dot strip to two opposite sides of the flower square and a $1\frac{1}{2}$" x $21\frac{1}{2}$" red/white polka-dot strip to the remaining sides to complete the pillow top.

3. Layer the pillow top with the 24" batting and muslin squares. Pin to hold together. Quilt as desired. Trim the batting and muslin lining even with the pillow top.

4. Fold the $21\frac{1}{2}$" x 28" red polka-dot floral rectangles in half to measure $21\frac{1}{2}$" x 14". Press.

5. Overlap the folded ends $3\frac{1}{4}$" and pin together to make the $21\frac{1}{2}$" square pillow back.

$3\frac{1}{4}$"

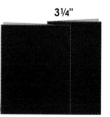

6. Place the quilted pillow top right side up on the pillow back. Pin to hold. Sew around the top $\frac{1}{8}$" from the outer edge.

7. Bind the edges using the binding left over from the quilt.

8. Insert the 20" pillow form to use.

Panel Pleaser Wall Quilt

Over the years I have designed more than a dozen fabric panels. I like to offer a fabric panel with each of my collections because it is a quick and easy way to make a wall quilt or lap quilt. Simply add borders and in no time at all you can make a quilt any size that you want.

Skill Level: Beginner
Finished quilt size: 31" x 49½"

SUPPLIES
Yardage is based on 42"-wide cotton fabric.
• One 22" x 38" flower-theme panel (Petal Pushers panel shown)
• Thirty-two 5" assorted charm squares
• ⅔ yd red basket-weave print
• 39" x 58" piece of backing fabric
• 39" x 58" piece of batting
• Thread in colors to match fabrics
• Rotary cutter, ruler and mat
• Basic sewing supplies

CUTTING INSTRUCTIONS
From the flower-theme panel, cut:
One 20½" x 37" rectangle

From the red basket-weave print, cut:
One 2½" x 42" strip; recut into two
    2½" x 20½" strips (border)
Two 1½" x 41½" strips (border)
Five 2½" x 42" strips (binding)

WALL QUILT ASSEMBLY AND FINISHING
Note: Refer to the quilt photo throughout. Use a ¼" seam allowance for all stitching. Sew all pieces with right sides together and raw edges aligned. Press seams toward the darker fabric after adding each piece or as indicated.

1. *Red Border.* Sew the 2½" x 20½" red basket-weave strips to the top and bottom of the panel and the 1½" x 41" red basket-weave strips to the sides. Press seams toward the strips.

2. *Pieced Border.* Lay out the charm squares around the bordered panel in two

sets of nine and two sets of seven to make a pleasing arrangement. Sew nine squares together to make a side strip. Repeat to make a second side strip. Sew to the sides of the quilt center. Sew seven squares together to make the top strip. Repeat to make the bottom strip. Sew to the top and bottom to complete the 31½" x 50" top. Press seams toward the strips.

3. Layer, quilt and bind using the five 2½" x 42" red basket-weave binding strips, referring to the Finishing Basics on page 93.

Chapter 2

Baby Boutique

As you walk through the shop, to the right you pass through what was once a bedroom in the original Victorian house. Now, one end of the room houses a collection of 1930s reproduction fabrics, as well as many Sunbonnet Sue samples that fill the area with the cheery colors of those wonderful feed-sack prints.

The other end of this area holds our Baby Boutique. The fabric collections here are designs that I have created over the last several years. The timeless soft baby flannels are filled with fanciful ducks, elephants, giraffes, turtles and friendly lions. What's not to love about making delightful darling baby quilts?

Blue Moon Baby Quilt & Block Pillow

Making rag-seam quilts can be quite addicting. This easy technique allows each block to be framed by clipping the seam allowances that are on the outside of the quilt. Once the body of the quilt is finished, simply machine wash and dry the quilt to get the fun, frayed seams. They are so soft—especially for babies.

Skill Level: Beginner
Finished quilt size: 46" x 55"
Block size sewn into quilt: 9" x 9"
Number of blocks: 20
Finished pillow size: 7" x 7" x 7"
Block size sewn into pillow: 7" x 7"
Number of blocks: 4

SUPPLIES

Yardage is based on 42"-wide unwashed cotton flannel.
- $2/3$ yard cream dot/blue flannel
- 1 yard white stars/yellow flannel
- 1 yard white stars/blue flannel
- $1^1/8$ yards cream dot/yellow flannel
- $1^1/4$ yards blue/yellow plaid flannel
- 3 yards blue tonal flannel
- $2^1/2$ yards 42"-wide batting
- Thread in colors to match fabrics
- Fiberfill stuffing
- Stiff-bristle brush
- Rotary cutter, ruler and mat
- Basic sewing supplies

CUTTING INSTRUCTIONS

From the cream dot/blue flannel, cut:
Ten large moon appliqué pieces

From the white stars/yellow flannel, cut:
Three 10" x 42" strips; recut into ten 10" squares
  and two 8" squares

From the white stars/blue flannel, cut:
Three 10" x 42" strips; recut into ten 10" squares
  and two 8" squares

From the cream dot/yellow flannel, cut:
One $5^3/4$" x 42" strip; recut into four $5^3/4$"
  squares (border)
Ten large star and two small star appliqué pieces

From the blue/yellow plaid flannel, cut:
Three $5^3/4$" x 42" strips (border)
Two $5^3/4$" x 37" strips (border)
Cut five $2^1/2$" x 42" strips (binding)

From the blue tonal flannel, cut:
Five 10" x 42" strips; recut into twenty 10"
  squares (backing)
One $5^3/4$" x 42" strip; recut into four $5^3/4$"
  squares (backing)
Three $5^3/4$" x 42" strips (backing)
Two $5^3/4$" x 37" strips (backing)
One 8" x 42" strip; recut into two 8" squares
Two small moon appliqué pieces

From the batting, cut:
Five 9" x 42" strips; recut into twenty 9" squares
Three $5^1/4$" x 42" strips
Two $5^1/4$" x 36" strips

INSTRUCTIONS

Moon and Star Blocks

1. Center a 9"x 9" square of batting on the wrong side of each 10" x 10" blue tonal backing square. Place a 10" x 10" white stars/yellow square right side up on 10 layered squares and a 10" x 10" white stars/blue square right side up on the remaining 10 layered squares.

2. Pin a large moon shape on the center of each yellow square and a large star shape on each blue square.

3. Sew the appliqués in place by topstitching $1/2$" from the edge inside the shapes to complete the blocks.

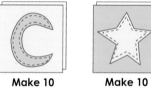

Make 10   Make 10

Borders

1. With right sides together and a $1/4$" seam allowance, sew three $5^3/4$" x 42" blue/yellow plaid strips short ends together to make a long strip. Press seams in one direction. Cut into two 46" lengths.

2. Repeat step 1 using three $5^3/4$" x 42" blue tonal strips to make backing strips.

3. Butt the ends of two $5^1/4$" x 42" batting strips. Slipstitch the ends together. Add the remaining $5^1/4$" x 42" strip. Cut two 45" lengths.

4. Place a 45" batting strip on the wrong side of a blue tonal 46" strip with one long edge aligned, $1/2$" from the ends.

5. Place a 46" blue/yellow plaid strip right side up on top. Pin to hold layers together. Repeat with the remaining 46" strips and the 45" batting strip to make two side border strips.

6. Repeat step 4 with the 5³/4" x 37" flannel strips and the 5¹/4" x 36" batting strips to make the top and bottom border strips.

7. Place a 5¹/4" batting square on the wrong side of a blue tonal 5³/4" square with two edges aligned.

8. Place a 5³/4" cream dot/yellow square on top. Pin to hold layers together. Repeat with remaining squares to make four border corner squares total.

QUILT ASSEMBLY AND FINISHING

Note: Refer to the Assembly Diagram throughout the following steps. Sew all pieces with backing sides together and edges aligned. Use a ¹/2" seam allowance throughout.

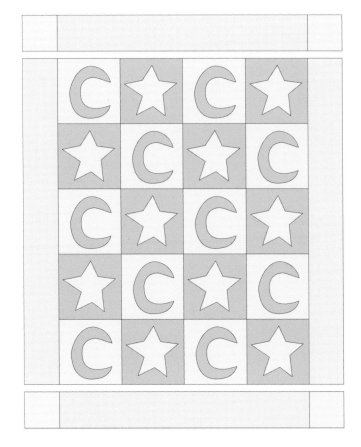

1. Arrange the blocks in five rows with four blocks in each row.

2. Place two blocks back to back. Sew along one edge using a ¹/2" seam allowance. Open the two blocks out with the seam on top.

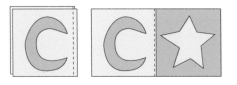

3. Continue to sew the blocks together to make five rows.

4. In the same manner, place two rows back to back and stitch together along one edge. Continue to join the rows to complete the 37" x 46" quilt center.

5. Place the edge, with no batting, of one side border strip back to back with one long edge of the quilt center. Sew along the edge. Open out with the seam on top. Repeat on the opposite long side of the quilt center.

6. In the same manner, sew a border corner square to each end of the top and bottom border strips with batting edges of the squares on the outside. Sew these strips to the top and bottom of the quilt center to complete the top.

7. Quilt the borders as desired.

8. Bind the edges using the five 2¹/2" x 42" blue/yellow plaid binding strips, referring to the Finishing Basics on page 93.

9. Clip all exposed seams every ¹/4" just to the stitched lines. Clip the edges of the appliqués every ¹/4" from the raw edge just to the stitched lines.

10. Wash the quilt in the washer. Dry the quilt in the dryer. Shake off the excess threads or remove with tape.

PILLOW ASSEMBLY AND FINISHING

Note: Sew all pieces with backing sides together and edges aligned. Use a ¹/2" seam allowance throughout.

1. Pin a small moon shape on each 8" white stars/yellow flannel square and a small star shape on each 8" white stars/blue flannel square. Topstitch in place ¹/2" from the edge of each appliqué shape.

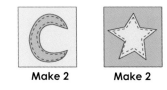

Make 2   Make 2

2. Sew a Moon block to a Star block to a Moon block to a Star block beginning and ending stitching ¹/2" from the corners.

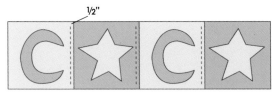

3. In the same manner, sew an 8" blue tonal square to opposite edges of the end Moon block.

4. Sew the adjacent edge of the blue tonal square to the top edge of the Star block.

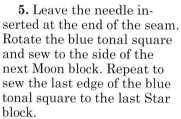

5. Leave the needle inserted at the end of the seam. Rotate the blue tonal square and sew to the side of the next Moon block. Repeat to sew the last edge of the blue tonal square to the last Star block.

6. Repeat to sew the edges of the remaining blue tonal square to the bottom edges of the Star, Moon and Star blocks to form a cube.

7. Align the open edges of the end Moon and Star blocks. Sew 2" from the top down and 2" up from the bottom, leaving an opening for stuffing.

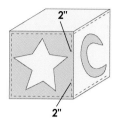

8. Stuff the block firmly.

9. Pin the opening closed. Stitch remainder of seam to complete the pillow.

10. Clip all seams every $1/4$" just to the stitched lines. Clip the edges of the appliqués every $1/4$" just to the stitched lines.

11. Dampen and brush each seam to fray the edges.

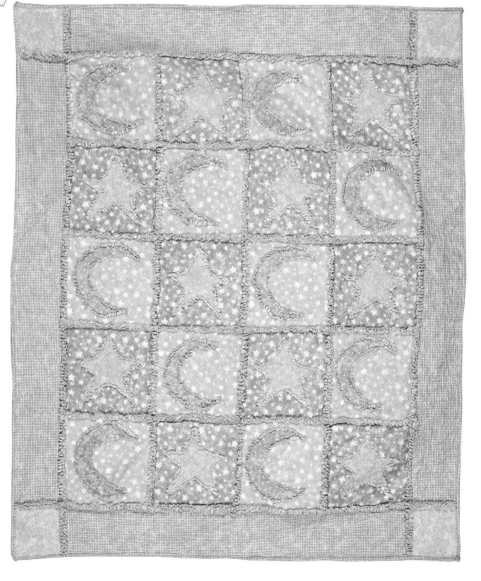

Blue Moon Tote

This lined baby tote is just the right size to carry the necessary items every mom and baby needs when they go out to shop or to visit friends and family.

Skill Level: Beginner
Finished tote size: 8" x 10" x 4"

SUPPLIES

Yardage is based on 42"-wide unwashed cotton flannel and fabric.
- 1/2 yard white stars/blue flannel
- 1/2 yard muslin
- 1 yard white stars/yellow flannel
- 5/8 yard 42"-wide batting
- Thread in colors to match fabrics
- Stiff-bristle brush
- Rotary cutter, ruler and mat
- Basic sewing supplies

CUTTING INSTRUCTIONS

From the white stars/blue flannel, cut:
One 8 1/2" x 42" strip; recut into two 8 1/2" x 10 1/2" front/back rectangles and one 6 1/2" x 8 1/2" pocket rectangle

One 4 1/2" x 42" strip; recut into two 4 1/2" x 10 1/2" side rectangles and one 4 1/2" x 8 1/2" bottom rectangle

From the muslin, cut:
One 14 1/2" x 42" strip

From the white stars/yellow flannel, cut:
One 14 1/2" x 42" strip
One 4 1/2" x 27" strip
Two 2 1/2" x 42" strips (binding)
One tote moon appliqué piece

From the batting, cut:
One 14 1/2" x 42" strip
One 2" x 26 1/2" strip

INSTRUCTIONS

Note: Use a 1/4" seam allowance throughout. Sew all pieces with right sides together and edges aligned.

Tote Sections

1. Place the 14½" x 42" batting strip between the same-size white stars/yellow strip and the muslin strip. Pin to hold together. Quilt as desired.

2. From the quilted strip, cut:
  Two 8½" x 10½" rectangles (front and back panels)
  Two 4½" x 10½" rectangles (side panels)
  One 4½" x 8½" rectangle (bottom)
  One 6½" x 8½" rectangle (front pocket)
  Two 4½" x 6½" rectangles (side pockets)

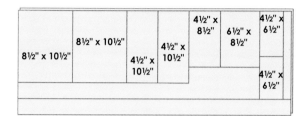

3. Place the 6½" x 8½" white stars/blue rectangle right side up on top of the 6½" x 8½" quilted front pocket rectangle. Stitch 1/4" from the edges all around.

4. Referring to Finishing Basics on page 93, prepare binding with one 2½" x 42" white stars/yellow strip. Bind one 8½" edge only of the front pocket and one 4½" edge of each of the two 4½" x 6½" quilted side pockets, stitching the binding to the muslin or white stars/yellow (back) sides of the rectangles. Trim binding to fit at ends. Turn the folded edge of the binding to the yellow (front) side of the pockets and hand-stitch in place.

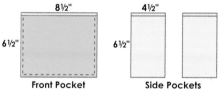

Front Pocket   Side Pockets

5. Pin the small moon appliqué shape on the blue side of the front pocket rectangle. Topstitch in place 1/4" inside the outer edge of the moon. Clip the edges of the moon every 1/4" just to the stitching line. Gently fray the outer edge of the moon using the stiff-bristle brush.

Clip edges

6. Pin the front pocket to the bottom 8½" edge of the 8½" x 10½" quilted front panel. Pin the side pockets to the bottom 4½" edges of the 4½" x 10½" quilted side panels.

Make 2

TOTE ASSEMBLY AND FINISHING

Note: Begin and end stitching 1/4" from the bottom corners of all pieces.

1. Lay out the tote sections as shown.

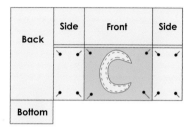

2. With right sides together, sew a side panel to one long edge of the back panel. Sew the front panel to the remaining side of the side panel, matching the top bound edges of the pockets. Sew the remaining side panel to the front panel.

3. With right sides together, sew one 8½" edge of the bottom panel to the bottom edge of the back panel. Leave the needle inserted.

4. Rotate and sew the bottom edge of the side panel to the narrow end of the bottom panel, leave the needle inserted. Rotate and sew the bottom panel to the bottom edge of the front panel. Sew the bottom edge of the remaining side panel to the bottom panel.

5. Sew the side seam to complete the tote shell. Turn right side out.

6. Repeat the above steps with the white stars/blue rectangles to make the tote lining, do not turn right side out.

7. Insert the lining in the tote shell with wrong sides together. Topstitch around the top 1/8" from the edge.

8. Use the remaining 2½" x 42" white stars/yellow strip to bind the top edge of the tote.

9. To make the tote handle, press one long edge and both short ends of the 4½" x 27" white stars/yellow strip 1/4" to the wrong side. Center the 2" x 26½" batting strip on the wrong side of the yellow strip.

Batting

10. Fold the outer edges of the yellow strip to the center covering the raw edge with the folded edge and enclosing the batting. Stitch along the long folded edge and across both ends.

11. Pin the ends of the strip to the inside of the tote side panels to make the handle. Machine-stitch in place to complete the tote.

Chapter 3

Tuscany Square

Several years ago I had the marvelous opportunity to travel to Italy. A very close designer friend asked me to join her and a group of other women on a group tour to several cities in Italy. When I was asked I wasn't very fond of the thought, but over several weeks I finally decided I could do this. The trip was truly one of the very best I have ever taken. I was filled with so much inspiration it was hard to choose what to design first. I finally chose to design a collection of fabrics entitled "Tuscany Square." This line features the rich colors of the Italy that I had enjoyed with my dear friend Sandy Dye.

I have created many samples with the Tuscany Square fabrics to fill the kitchen area of the shop. This is the room where we hold Thimble Thursday classes. Each Thursday at 1:00 p.m., our Thimble Thursday ladies come to enjoy the gathering of quilting friends. We provide the treats. They provide a show and tell, and then they receive a kit for a project that all of the members create. The kitchen gets a little crowded with over 20 members but everyone has a great time.

Sunflower Table Topper

Place this pieced and machine appliquéd table topper on your dining or kitchen table and you have just created a new theme for your room. Consider quilting this topper with a variegated thread that will accent the fabrics.

Skill Level: Beginner
Finished topper size: 38" x 38"
Block size sewn into topper: 8" x 8"
Number of blocks: 9

SUPPLIES
Yardage is based on 42"-wide cotton fabric.
- 1/4 yard light yellow print
- 1/4 yard medium gold print
- 1/4 yard brown swirl print
- 1/3 yard white/cream print
- 3/8 yard gold floral print
- 3/8 yard red tonal print
- 3/4 yard green swirl print
- 7/8 yard gold plaid
- 46" x 46" piece of backing fabric
- 46" x 46" piece of batting
- Thread in colors to match fabrics
- 3/4 yard 18"-wide fusible web
- Rotary cutter, ruler and mat
- Basic sewing supplies

CUTTING INSTRUCTIONS
From the light yellow print and medium gold print, cut:
Appliqué pieces as per instructions

From the brown swirl print, cut:
One 11/2" x 42" strip; recut into sixteen 11/2" squares
Appliqué pieces as per instructions

From the white/cream print, cut:
One 81/2" x 42 " strip; recut into four 81/2" squares

From the gold floral print, cut:
One 41/2" x 42" strip
Two 21/2" x 42" strips

From the red tonal print, cut:
Six 11/2" x 42" strips; recut into twenty-four 11/2" x 81/2" strips

From the green swirl print, cut:
Two 11/2" x 281/2" strips (border)
Two 11/2" x 301/2" strips (border)
Two 11/2" x 361/2" strips (border)
Two 11/2" x 381/2" strips (border)
Four 21/2" x 42" strips (binding)

From the gold plaid, cut:
One 41/2" x 42" strip
Two 21/2" x 42" strips
Two 31/2" x 30 1/2" strips (border)
Two 31/2" x 361/2" strips (border)

INSTRUCTIONS
Note: Use a 1/4" seam allowance throughout. Sew all pieces with right sides together and edges aligned. Press seams toward the darker fabric after adding each piece or as indicated.

Nine Patch Blocks
1. Sew the 41/2" x 42" gold floral strip lengthwise between two 21/2" x 42" gold plaid strips. Press seams toward the plaid strips. Crosscut the strip set into ten 21/2" segments.

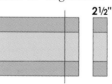

2. Sew the 41/2" x 42" gold plaid strip lengthwise between two 21/2" x 42" gold floral strips. Press seam toward the plaid strip. Crosscut the strip set into five 41/2" segments.

3. Sew a 4¹/₂" segment between two 2¹/₂" segments to complete one 8¹/₂" x 8¹/₂" block. Press seams toward the center strip. Repeat to make a total of five blocks.

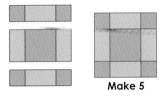

Make 5

Sunflower Blocks

Note: Refer to the basic instructions for Fusible Appliqué on page 92 to prepare Sunflower blocks.

1. Prepare fusible appliqué pieces for the sunflower and center using the patterns given in the pull-out pattern section.

2. Fuse one flower motif on each 8¹/₂" white/cream print square. Use a decorative stitch and thread to match fabrics to complete four 8¹/₂" x 8¹/₂" blocks.

QUILT ASSEMBLY AND FINISHING

Note: Refer to the Assembly Diagram throughout the following steps. Press seams toward each border strip as added.

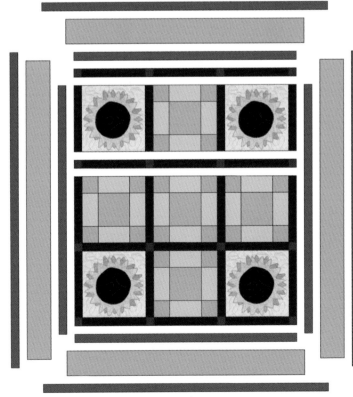

Assembly Diagram

1. Sew four 1¹/₂" brown swirl sashing squares alternately together with three 1¹/₂" x 8¹/₂" red tonal strips to make a sashing row. Press seams toward the strips. Repeat to make a total of four rows.

2. Stitch three blocks alternately together with four 1¹/₂" x 8¹/₂" red tonal strips to make a block row. Press seams toward the strips. Repeat to make a total of three block rows.

3. Sew the sashing rows alternately with the block rows to complete the 28¹/₂" x 28¹/₂" topper center.

4. *Inner Border* Sew a 1¹/₂" x 28¹/₂" green swirl strip to two sides of the topper center. Sew a 1¹/₂" x 30¹/₂" green swirl strip to the remaining sides.

5. *Middle Border* Sew a 3¹/₂" x 30¹/₂" gold plaid strip to two sides of the topper center. Sew a 3¹/₂" x 36¹/₂" gold plaid strip to the remaining sides.

6. *Outer Border* Sew a 1¹/₂" x 36¹/₂" green swirl strip to two sides of the topper center. Sew a 1¹/₂" x 38¹/₂" green swirl strip to the remaining sides.

7. Layer, quilt and bind the table topper using the four 2¹/₂" x 42" green swirl binding strips, referring to the Finishing Basics on page 93.

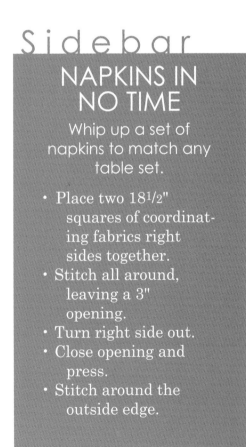

Sunflower Potholders

Adding potholders to any kitchen collection is both fun and functional. These potholders use the sunflower block included in the table topper.

Skill Level: Beginner
Pot holder finished size: 8" x 8"
Number of potholders: 2

SUPPLIES
Yardage is based on 42"-wide cotton fabric.
- 1/4 yard medium gold print
- 1/4 yard light gold print
- 1/4 yard brown swirl print
- 1/4 yard green swirl print
- 1/3 yard white/cream print
- 1/3 yard gold plaid
- 1/2 yard 42"-wide cotton or heat-resistant batting
- Thread in colors to match fabrics
- 1/2 yard fusible web
- Rotary cutter, ruler and mat
- Basic sewing supplies

CUTTING INSTRUCTIONS
From the medium gold print, light gold print and brown swirl print, cut:
Appliqué pieces as per instructions

From the green swirl print, cut:
Two 2 1/2" x 42" strips (binding)

From the white/cream print, cut:
Two 8 1/2" squares

From the gold plaid print, cut:
Two 8 1/2" squares

From the batting, cut:
Four 8 1/2" squares

INSTRUCTIONS

Note: Use a ¼" seam allowance throughout. Press seams toward the darker fabric after adding each piece or as indicated.

POTHOLDER ASSEMBLY

Note: Refer to the basic instructions for Fusible Appliqué on page 92 to prepare sunflower squares.

1. Prepare fusible appliqué pieces for the sunflower and center using the patterns given in the pull-out pattern section.

2. Fuse one flower motif on each 8½" white/cream print square. Use a decorative stitch and thread to match fabrics to complete two sunflower squares.

3. Place two batting squares on the wrong side of one 8½" gold plaid square. Place the sunflower square right side up on top. Pin layers together. Repeat with the remaining squares.

4. Prepare binding using the 2½" x 42" green swirl strips and bind the edges of the layered squares referring to the Finishing Basics on page 93.

5. Stitch around the sunflower center and petals to quilt the layers and to finish the potholders.

Village Gatherings

When I first opened the Thimble Cottage Quilt Shop, I planned to have many clubs and classes. I wanted to teach and inspire our customers, who have always inspired me. One of the first classes I organized was Thimble Thursday. This club has been meeting for more than 15 years. It has grown to become a wonderful gathering of friends, who share their quilts and other interests during the lecture-style meetings. A kit with instructions is provided for each Thimble Thursday meeting.

I have held many School House events here at the Thimble Cottage Quilt Village and at a local bed and breakfast. For each event, we invite several teachers to come and demonstrate their favorite quilting techniques. Each teacher uses a different room. Classes begin in the morning. Lunch and dessert are served before continuing with afternoon classes. These events are always well received. Once we organized a mystery quilt class that was held at a local campground called Mystery Mountain. It was a huge success.

Chapter 4

Quilters' Heaven

When you cross through the foyer to the other side of the Thimble Cottage, you can enter both the classroom/design room and the cutting room. The cutting room is the fabric gallery; the walls and center of the space are lined with many collections of beautiful quilting fabrics. The color wall contains many basics, and the other displays hold collections of different themed fabrics.

There isn't much room in this space for stitched samples to be displayed. In fact, most of the wall space holds several table topper samples. Many of these toppers were made in our Dinner and Design classes. Our Dinner and Design members pay for a kit, class and dinner for each session. After dinner is served and dessert is enjoyed, the ladies come to the classroom to work on the table accessories featured in this chapter. I hope you enjoy them as much as our members have.

Tuscan Garden Table Runner

When you first look at this runner you may think it is difficult to make. But once you break down the simple block sections, this runner is easy to piece and will add drama to any dining area.

Skill Level: Beginner
Finished runner size: 18" x 46"
Block size sewn into runner: 12" x 12"
Number of blocks: 3

SUPPLIES

Yardage is based on 42"-wide cotton fabric.
- 1/4 yard small black/red floral
- 1/3 yard green print
- 1/2 yard medium black/red floral
- 1/2 yard light tan print
- 5/8 yard red dot
- 26" x 54" piece of backing
- 26" x 54" piece of batting
- Thread in colors to match fabrics
- Rotary cutter, ruler and mat
- Basic sewing supplies

CUTTING INSTRUCTIONS

From the small black/red floral, cut:
Four 1¹/₂" x 42" strips; recut into twenty-four
    1¹/₂" x 2¹/₂" rectangles and forty-eight
    1¹/₂" squares

From the green print, cut:
One 2¹/₂" x 42" strip; recut into five 2¹/₂" squares
Three 1¹/₂" x 42" strips; recut into twelve
    1¹/₂" x 4¹/₂" rectangles and twelve 1¹/₂" x
    5¹/₂" rectangles

From the medium black/red floral, cut:
One 2¹/₂" x 42" strip; recut into twelve 2¹/₂"
    squares
One 2¹/₂" x 42" strip; recut into two 2¹/₂" x
    18¹/₂" strips (border)
Three 2¹/₂" x 42" strips (border)

From the light tan print, cut:
Three 2¹/2" x 42" strips; recut into sixteen 2¹/2"
x 5¹/2" rectangles and twelve 2¹/2" squares
Three 1¹/2" x 42" strips; recut into twenty-four
1¹/2" x 2¹/2" rectangles and twenty-four
1¹/2" squares

From the red dot, cut:
Two 1¹/2" x 40¹/2" strips (border)
One 1¹/2" x 42" strip; recut into two 1¹/2" x
14¹/2" strips (border)
Four 2¹/2" x 42" strips (binding)

INSTRUCTIONS
Note: Use a ¹/4" seam allowance throughout. Sew
all pieces with right sides together and edges
aligned. Press seams toward the darker fabric
after adding each piece or as indicated.

Garden Square Block
1. Draw a diagonal line across the wrong side
of the 1¹/2" light tan print and small black/red
floral squares.
2. Place a marked black/red floral square right
sides together on one end of each 1¹/2" x 2¹/2" light
tan rectangle. Sew on the marked lines. Trim
seam allowances to ¹/4" and press the floral
corners to the right side.

Make 24

3. Repeat step 2 on the remaining end of the
light tan rectangles to complete twenty-four
flying geese units.

Make 24

4. Sew a 1¹/2" x 2¹/2" small black/red floral
rectangle to each flying geese unit.

Make 24

5. Sew a 2¹/2" light tan square to twelve pieced
units and a 2¹/2" medium black/red floral square
to the twelve remaining pieced units. Sew one of
each pieced unit together to make a flower unit.
Repeat to make a total of twelve flower units.

Make 12

6. Place a marked 1¹/2" light tan square right
sides together on one end of each 1¹/2" x 4¹/2" and
1¹/2" x 5¹/2" green rectangle. Sew on the marked
lines. Trim seam allowances to ¹/4" and press
the light tan corners to the right side to complete
leaf strips.

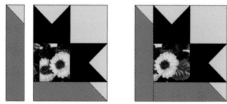
Make 12
Make 12

7. Sew a 4¹/2" leaf strip to one black side of
each flower unit and a 5¹/2" leaf strip to the
remaining black side to complete twelve block
units.

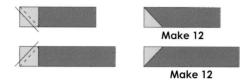

8. Sew a 2¹/2" x 5¹/2" light tan rectangle
between two block units to make a side row.
Press seams toward the light tan rectangles.
Repeat to make a second side row.

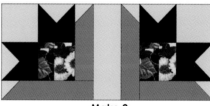
Make 2

9. Sew a 2¹/2" green square between two 2¹/2" x
5¹/2" light tan rectangles to make the center row.
Press seams toward the light tan rectangles.

10. Sew the center row between the side rows
to complete one 12¹/2" x 12¹/2" block. Press seams
toward the center row. Repeat to make a total of
three blocks.

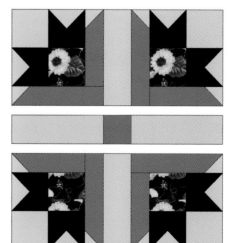
Make 3

TABLE RUNNER ASSEMBLY

Note: Refer to the Assembly Diagram throughout the following steps. Press seams toward each border strip as added.

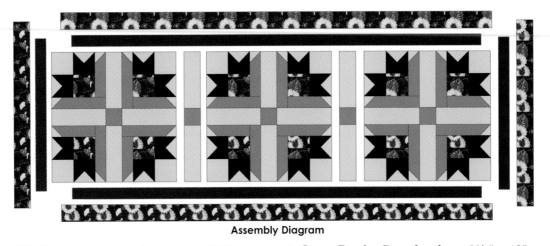

Assembly Diagram

1. Sew a 2½" green square between two 2½" x 5½" light tan rectangles to make a sashing strip. Press seams toward the light tan rectangles. Repeat to make a second sashing strip.

2. Sew the blocks alternately together with the sashing strips to complete the 12½" x 40½" runner center. Press seams toward the sashing strips.

3. *Inner Border* Sew a 1½" x 40½" red dot strip to the long sides and the 1½" x 14½" strips to the ends of the center.

4. *Outer Border* Sew the three 2½" x 42" medium black/red floral strips short ends together to make a long strip. Cut into two 42½" lengths. (**Note:** Measure your strips before stitching. Your fabric may yield 42½" strips without piecing.) Sew a strip to the long sides of the runner center. Sew a 2½" x 18½" medium black/red floral to the ends to complete the runner top.

5. Layer, quilt and bind the runner using the three 2½" x 42" red dot binding strips, referring to the Finishing Basics on page 93.

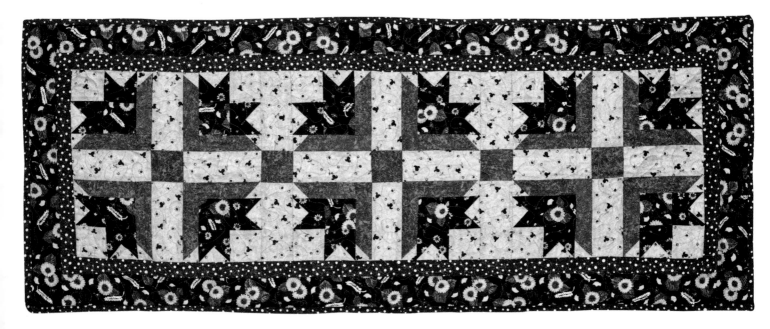

Pinwheel Magic Table Runner

Choose fabrics to match your dinnerware to create this easy table runner.
Your friends and family will be delighted with the results.

Skill Level: Beginner
Finished runner size: 17" x 37"
Block size sewn into runner: 9" x 9"
Number of blocks: 3

SUPPLIES

Yardage is based on 42"-wide cotton fabric.
• Fat quarter blue paisley print
• 1/4 yard blue print
• 1/3 yard gold print
• 3/8 yard tan print
• 1/2 yard blue stripe
• 25" x 45" piece of backing
• 25" x 45" piece of batting
• Thread in colors to match fabrics
• Rotary cutter, ruler and mat
• Basic sewing supplies

CUTTING INSTRUCTIONS

From the blue paisley print, cut:
Three 2³/4" x 21" strips; recut into twelve
    2³/4" x 5" rectangles
One 1¹/2" x 21" strip; recut into eight 1¹/2"
    squares
One 2" x 21" strip; recut into eight 2" squares

From the blue print, cut:
Three 2" x 42" strips; recut into two 2" x 31¹/2"
    strips and two 2" x 11¹/2" strips (border)

From the gold print, cut:
Three 1¹/2" x 42" strips; recut into ten 1¹/2" x
    9¹/2" rectangles
One 2³/4" x 42" strip; recut into twelve 2³/4"
    squares

From the tan print, cut:
Three 2³/4" x 42" strips; recut into twelve 2³/4"
    x 5 rectangles and twelve 2³/4" squares

From the blue stripe, cut:
Three 2" x 42" strips; recut into two 2" x 34¹/2"
    strips and two 2" x 14¹/2" strips (border)
Three 2¹/2" x 42" strips (binding)

INSTRUCTIONS
Note: Use a ¹/4" seam allowance throughout. Sew
all pieces with right sides together and edges
aligned. Press seams toward the darker fabric
after adding each piece or as indicated.

Pinwheel Blocks
1. Draw a diagonal line across the wrong side
of the 2³/4" tan print and gold print squares.
2. Place a marked gold square right sides together on one end of each 2³/4" x 5" blue paisley
rectangle. Sew on the marked lines. Trim seam
allowances to ¹/4" and press the gold corners to
the right side.

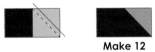

Make 12

3. Repeat step 2 with a 2³/4" tan square on the
remaining end of each blue paisley rectangle to
complete twelve flying geese units.

Make 12

4. Sew a 2³/4" x 5" tan print rectangle to
one side of each flying geese unit to complete
twelve block units. Press seams toward the tan
rectangles.

Make 12

5. Arrange four block units to make a block.
Sew two units together to make a row. Repeat
with the remaining two units. Sew the two rows
together to complete one 9¹/2" x 9¹/2" block.
Repeat to make a total of three blocks.

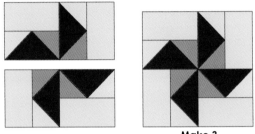

Make 3

TABLE RUNNER ASSEMBLY
Note: Refer to the Assembly Diagram throughout
the following steps. Press seams toward each
border strip as added.

Assembly Diagram

1. Sew the three blocks alternately together with four 1¹/₂" x 9¹/₂" gold print strips to complete the block row. Press seams toward the gold strips.

2. Sew three 1¹/₂" x 9¹/₂" gold print strips alternately together with four 1¹/₂" blue paisley squares to make a sashing row. Press seams toward the gold strips. Repeat to make a second sashing row.

3. Sew the sashing rows to the long sides of the block row to complete the 11¹/₂" x 31¹/₂" runner center. Press seams toward the sashing rows.

4. *Inner Border* Sew a 2" x 31¹/₂" blue print strip to the long sides of the center. Sew a 2" blue paisley square to each end of the two 2" x 11¹/₂" blue print strips. Sew these strips to the ends of the center.

5. *Outer Border* Sew a 2" x 34¹/₂" blue stripe strip to the long sides of the center. Sew a 2" blue paisley square to each end of the two 2" x 14¹/₂" blue stripe strips. Sew these strips to the ends of the center to complete the top.

6. Layer, quilt and bind the runner using the three 2¹/₂" x 42" blue stripe binding strips, referring to the Finishing Basics on page 93.

s i d e b a r

Add Placemats
Complete your table set with easy matching placemats.

For the Pinwheel Magic runner:
- Make an extra block for each place mat.
- Add a sashing strip to the sides of the block, but not to the top and bottom.
- Add borders to match the runner.

For the Tuscan Garden Runner:
- Make an extra block for each place mat.
- Add a red dot border to the sides of the block, but not to the top and bottom.
- Add a floral border all around to match the runner.

Bind the placemats as you did the runner to complete the set.

Sew Easy Kitchen Collection

This collection of "quilt-as-you-go" placemats and potholders can be made in an evening. They make a great accent in any kitchen and also great gifts or bazaar items.

Skill Level: Beginner
Placemat finished size: 12" x 18"
Number of placemats: 4
Potholder finished size: 6" x 9"
Number of potholders: 2

SUPPLIES
Yardage is based on 42"-wide cotton fabric.
- Fat quarter olive swirl print
- Fat quarter copper swirl print
- 1/3 yard tan berry print
- 1/3 yard olive plaid
- 1 yard brown swirl print
- 1 3/4 yards copper pinecone print
- 1 5/8 yards 42"-wide cotton or heat-resistant batting
- Thread in colors to match fabrics
- Walking foot
- Rotary cutter, ruler and mat
- Basic sewing supplies

CUTTING INSTRUCTIONS
From the olive swirl print, cut:
Two 2 1/2" x 21 strips; recut into eight 2 1/2" x 4 1/2" rectangles
One 1 1/2" x 21" strip; recut into four 1 1/2" x 2 1/2" rectangles

From the copper swirl print, cut:
One 4 1/2" x 21" strip; recut into four 4 1/2" x 4 1/2" squares
One 2 1/2" x 21" strip; recut into two 2 1/2" x 2 1/2" squares

From the tan berry print, cut:
Two 2 1/2" x 42" strips; recut into eight 2 1/2" x 8 1/2" rectangles
One 1 1/2" x 42" strip; recut into four 1 1/2" x 4 1/2" rectangles

From the olive plaid, cut:
Two 2 1/2" x 42" strips; recut into eight 2 1/2" x 8 1/2" rectangles
One 1 1/2" x 42" strip; recut into four 1 1/2" x 4 1/2" rectangles

From the brown swirl print, cut:
Three 2 1/2" x 42" strips; recut into eight 2 1/2" x 12 1/2" rectangles and two 2" x 5" strips
One 1 1/2" x 42" strip; recut into four 1 1/2" x 6 1/2" rectangles
Eight 2 1/2" x 42" strips (binding)

From the copper pinecone print, cut:
Three 3 1/2" x 42" strips; recut into eight 3 1/2" x 12 1/2" rectangles
One 2" x 42" strip; recut into four 2" x 6 1/2" rectangles
Two 22" x 42" strips; recut into four 16" x 22" rectangles and two 7" x 10" rectangles

From the batting, cut:
Two 22" x 40" strips; recut into four 16" x 22" rectangles (placemats)
One 7" x 40" strip; recut into four 7" x 10" rectangles (potholders)

INSTRUCTIONS
Note: Use a 1/4" seam allowance throughout. Sew all pieces with right sides together and edges aligned. Press seams away from the center squares.

PLACEMAT ASSEMBLY AND FINISHING
1. Fold the 4 1/2" copper swirl squares in half twice and press to mark the center. Unfold. Repeat with the 16" x 22" copper pinecone rectangles.

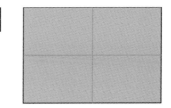

2. Place a copper pinecone rectangle wrong side up. Layer a 16" x 22" batting rectangle on top.
3. Push a straight pin through the creased center point of the 4 1/2" copper square. Place the square on the layered rectangles, pushing the pin through the creased center point of the rectangle to align the pieces. Pin the layers together to hold.

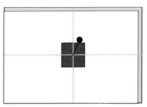

4. Repeat steps 2 and 3 with the remaining copper squares, rectangles and batting.

5. Sew a 2½" x 4½" olive swirl rectangle to the top and bottom of the copper squares. Press.

6. Sew a 2½" x 8½" tan berry print rectangle to the long sides of the pieced section. Press.

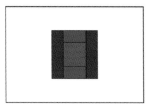

7. In this same manner, add the 2½" x 8½" olive plaid rectangles to the top and bottom and the 3½" x 12½" copper pinecone rectangles to the sides. Sew the 2½" x 12½" brown swirl rectangles to the sides to complete the placemat tops.

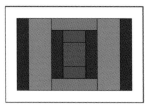

8. Trim the batting and backing even with the placemat tops.

9. Bind the edges of the placemats using the eight 2½" x 42" brown swirl binding strips, referring to the Finishing Basics on page 93. Set aside the remaining binding for the pot holders.

POTHOLDER ASSEMBLY AND FINISHING

1. Repeat steps 1–4 of the placemat instructions using the 2½" copper swirl squares, 7" x 10" copper pinecone/bird rectangles and 7" x 10" batting rectangles. Layer two batting rectangles for each potholder.

Tip: Apply a bit of basting spray between the batting rectangles and the fabric backing to hold the thick layers of the potholder together. This will prevent slipping as the fabric strips are stitched to the top.

2. Repeat steps 5–9 of the placemat instructions using the 1½" x 2½" olive swirl rectangles, 1½" x 4½" tan berry print rectangles, 1½" x 4½" olive plaid rectangles, 2" x 6½" copper pinecone/bird rectangles and 1½" x 6½" brown swirl rectangles.

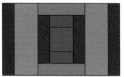

3. To make the hanging loops, turn each short end of the 2" x 5" brown swirl strips ¼" to the wrong side. Fold the strips in half along the length and crease the center. Fold the long raw edges of the strips to the creased center. Press. Fold the strips in half on the creased centerline. Press. Topstitch along the folded edge and across each end.

4. Fold each strip in half to form a loop. Stitch across the ends to hold. Stitch a loop to a back corner of each potholder to finish.

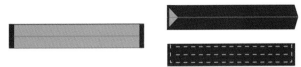

Village Gatherings

The First Saturday Club is another class that we offer. Each year I design a new quilt that is broken down into twelve steps. Our class members receive a pattern and demonstration of the block or section of the quilt. They are required to finish that section before the next meeting or they are charged a small fee to continue. This year we are in the process of building paper-pieced blocks. This technique is new to most of our members but they are all completing their blocks and are excited to see what is coming next. Last year the quilt was in the round-robin style.

Block of the Month designs have become my all time favorite type of quilt to create. Many photos throughout this book show the block of the month quilts. One of the most popular themes for these quilts is snowmen. We have several different Snowmen Block of the Month Quilts, such as The Blizzard Bunch, The Hot Chocolate Club, Family Reunion, Chilly Charmers, and The Snow Sweet Shoppe, displayed throughout the Thimble Cottage Quilt Village. We also have the spring and s ummer block of the month quilt patterns, Nesting, Blessings, The Guildy Girls Garden Club, The Village Mystery and Petal Pushers. We bundle fabrics to coordinate with the patterns as requested by our visitors.

Chapter 5

Pieces of Time

As you make your way through the cutting room there is a small hallway that was a main entrance when the building was the Dinosaur Hotel. The hall connects the cutting room and the classroom, which also houses more fabric, the design area and the production area. This is where many messes are made and where all of the major designing and pattern production takes place. This is also where we hold our First Saturday Classes. There are always new samples displayed in this area. The project for this room is a very basic and charming sampler throw quilt made in three different color ways.

Pieces of Time Sampler Quilt

The quilt blocks used in this sampler are traditional blocks with a few new techniques to make the construction easier. This is a chance to create many quilt blocks that we all remember. Put them together in a lap or wall quilt to make friends and family feel welcome.

Skill Level: Intermediate
Finished quilt size: 62" x 76"
Block size sewn into quilt: 12" x 12"
Number of blocks: 12

SUPPLIES

Yardage is based on 42"-wide cotton fabric.
- Fat eighth pink print
- 1/4 yard red solid
- 1/2 yard medium brown dot
- 2/3 yard multicolor print
- 3/4 yard tan print
- 1 yard red dot
- 1 1/8 yards medium blue print
- 1 1/8 yards medium brown print
- 1 1/4 yards blue stripe
- 1 3/4 yards dark blue print
- 2 yards total cream/white prints
- 70" x 84" piece of backing fabric
- 70" x 84" piece of batting
- Thread in colors to match fabrics
- 1/4 yard fusible web
- Template material
- Card stock
- Spray starch
- Fine-point pencil
- Rotary cutter, mat and ruler
- Basic sewing supplies

CUTTING INSTRUCTIONS FOR SASHING, BORDERS AND BINDING

Note: Cutting instructions are given separately for each block. See individual block sections.

From the red solid, cut:
Two 2 1/2" x 42" strips; recut into twenty 2 1/2" squares

From the medium brown print, cut:
Eleven 2 1/2" x 42" strips; recut into thirty-one 2 1/2" x 12 1/2" strips
One 6 1/2" x 42" strip; recut into four 6 1/2" squares (border)

From the dark blue print, cut:
Six 1 1/2" x 42" strips (border)
Seven 2 1/2" x 42" strips (border)
Seven 2 1/2" x 42" strips (binding)

From the blue stripe, cut:
Six 6 1/2" x 42" strips (border)

GENERAL INSTRUCTIONS

Note: Instructions and cutting are given for the blue/red/tan version of the sampler quilt.
1. Use a 1/4" seam allowance throughout.
2. Sew all pieces with right sides together and edges aligned.
3. Press seams toward the darker fabric after adding each piece or as indicated.
4. Prepare templates for A, B, C, and D using patterns given in the pull-out pattern section. Draw the centerline on the B template and make a small hole in the template at each corner dot.

SAWTOOTH STAR

Cutting
Multicolor print:
One 6 1/2" x 6 1/2" square
Tan print:
Four 3 1/2" x 3 1/2" squares
Cream/white print:
Eight 3 1/2" x 3 1/2" squares
Medium blue print:
Four 3 1/2" x 6 1/2" rectangles
Four 3 1/2" x 3 1/2" squares

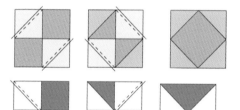

Make 4

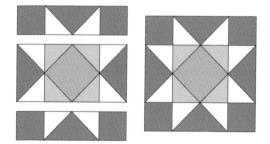

1. Draw a diagonal line across the wrong side of the 3 1/2" tan and cream/white squares.
2. Place a marked tan square right sides together on opposite corners of the 6 1/2" multicolor square. Sew on the marked lines. Trim leaving a 1/4" seam allowance. Open and press toward the tan corners. Repeat on the remaining corners to complete the center square.

3. Place a marked 3½" cream/white square right sides together on one end of each 3½" x 6½" medium blue rectangle. Sew on the marked lines. Trim leaving a ¼" seam allowance. Open and press toward the cream/white corners. Repeat on the remaining end of the rectangles to complete four side units.

4. Sew a side unit to two opposite sides of the center square. Press seams toward the center square. Sew a 3½" medium blue square to each end of the two remaining side units. Press seams toward the squares. Sew a strip to the remaining sides of the center square to complete the 12½" x 12½" block. Press seams away from the block center.

DOUBLE NINE PATCH

Cutting
Red dot:
Four 4½" x 4½" squares
Dark blue print:
Twenty-five template A pieces
Cream/white print:
Twenty template A pieces

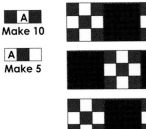
Make 10

Make 5

1. Sew a cream/white A piece between two dark blue A pieces. Repeat to make ten side strips. Sew a dark blue A piece between two cream/white A pieces. Repeat to make five center strips.

2. Sew a center strip between two side strips to complete one Nine-Patch unit. Press seams toward the side strips. Repeat to make a total of five units.

4. Sew a Nine-Patch unit between two 4½" red dot squares to make the center row. Press seams toward the squares. Sew a 4½" red dot square between two Nine-Patch units to make a side row. Press seams toward the square. Repeat to make a second side row. Sew the center row between the side rows to complete the 12½" x 12½" block.

CONTRARY WIFE

Cutting
Medium blue print:
Five 4½" x 4½" squares
Medium brown dot:
Two 4⅞" x 4⅞" squares
Cream/white print:
Two 4⅞" x 4⅞" squares

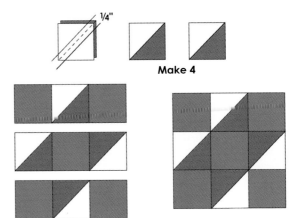
Make 4

1. Draw a diagonal line across the wrong side of the 4⅞" cream/white squares.

2. Place a marked square right sides together on a medium brown square. Sew a ¼" seam on each side of the marked line. Cut apart on the marked line. Open and press toward the medium brown side to make two cream/brown units. Repeat to make a total of four units.

3. Sew a cream/brown unit between two 4½" medium blue squares to make a side row. Press seams toward the squares. Repeat to make a second side row. Sew a 4½" medium blue square between two cream/brown units to make the center row. Press seams toward the square. Sew the center row between the side rows to complete the 12½" x 12½" block. Press seams toward the side rows.

SISTER'S CHOICE

Cutting
Multicolor print:
Four 3½" x 3½" squares
Eight 2½" x 2½" squares
Cream/white print:
Four 2½" x 2½" squares
Eight 2½" x 3½" rectangles
Tan print:
Four 2½" x 3½" rectangles
Medium brown dot:
Five 2½" x 2½" squares

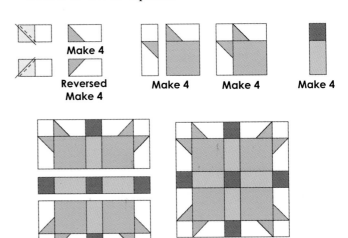
Make 4

Reversed
Make 4

Make 4

Make 4

Make 4

1. Draw a diagonal line across the wrong side of the 2 1/2" multicolor squares.

2. Place a marked square right sides together on one end of each 2 1/2" x 3 1/2" cream/white rectangle. Sew on the marked lines. Trim leaving a 1/4" seam allowance. Open and press toward the cream/white corners to make four side units and four reverse side units.

3. Sew a side unit to one side of a 3 1/2" multicolor square. Press seam toward the square. Sew a 2 1/2" cream/white square to a reverse side unit. Press seam toward the square. Sew the two pieced units together to make a corner unit. Press seam in one direction. Repeat to make a total of four corner units.

4. Sew a 2 1/2" medium brown dot square to a 2 1/2" x 3 1/2" tan rectangle. Repeat to make a total of four pieced strips.

5. Sew the remaining 2 1/2" medium brown dot square between two pieced strips to make the center row. Press seams toward the pieced strips. Sew a pieced strip between two corner units to make a side row. Press seams toward the pieced strip. Repeat to make a second side row. Sew the center row between the side rows to complete the 12 1/2" x 12 1/2" block. Press seams toward the center row.

SCHOOLHOUSE

Cutting

Red dot:
Two 1 1/2" x 5 1/2" strips
Three 1 1/2" x 3 1/2" strips
Two 1 1/2" x 2 1/2" strips
Three 2 1/2" x 5 1/2" rectangles
Two 2 1/2" x 2 1/2" squares
One 2 7/8" x 2 7/8" square
One 3 1/2" x 4 1/2" rectangle

Medium brown dot:
One 1 1/2" x 12 1/2" strip
Two 1 1/2" x 3 1/2" rectangles

Tan print:
One 2 1/2" x 5 1/2" rectangle
One 2 1/2" x 3 1/2" rectangle
One 1 1/2" x 7 1/2" strip
One 1 1/2" x 6 1/2" strip

Medium blue print:
Two 1 1/2" x 11 1/2" strips
Three 1 1/2" x 2 1/2" strips
One 2 7/8" x 2 7/8" square
One 2 1/2" x 2 1/2" square

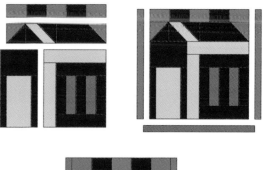

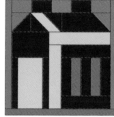

1. Draw a diagonal line across the wrong side of the 2 7/8" medium blue square, the 2 1/2" medium blue square and the 2 1/2" red dot squares.

2. Place the marked 2 7/8" square right sides together on the 2 7/8" red dot square. Sew a 1/4" seam on each side of the drawn line. Cut apart on the drawn line. Open and press toward the blue side to make two triangle units. Set aside one unit for another project or discard.

3. Place a marked 2 1/2" red square right sides together on one end of the 2 1/2" x 3 1/2" tan rectangle. Sew on the marked line. Trim leaving a 1/4" seam allowance. Open and press toward the red corner. Repeat on the remaining end of the rectangle. Repeat with the marked 2 1/2" medium blue square on one end of a 2 1/2" x 5 1/2" red dot rectangle.

4. Sew the units pieced in steps 2 and 3 together to make the roof section. Press seams toward the red pieces.

5. Sew two 1 1/2" x 2 1/2" red rectangles together with three 1 1/2" x 2 1/2" medium blue rectangles to make the sky section. Press seams toward the red rectangles.

6. Sew the 2 1/2" x 5 1/2" tan rectangle between two 1 1/2" x 5 1/2" red strips and add the 3 1/2" x 4 1/2" red rectangle to one end to complete the door section. Press seams toward the red pieces.

7. Sew the 1 1/2" x 3 1/2" medium brown strips together with the 1 1/2" x 3 1/2" red strips and add a 2 1/2" x 5 1/2" red rectangle to the top and bottom. Press seams toward the red pieces. Add the 1 1/2" x 7 1/2" tan strip to one side and the 1 1/2" x 6 1/2" tan strip to the top to complete the window section. Press seams toward the red pieces.

1/4"   Make 1   Make 1

8. Sew the door section to the window section. Press seam toward the door section. Sew the sky section to the roof section. Press seam toward the sky section. Sew the two pieced sections together to complete the house section. Press seams toward the door/window section.

9. Sew a 1¹/₂" x 11¹/₂" medium blue strip to two opposite sides and the 1¹/₂" x 12¹/₂" medium brown strip to the bottom of the house section to complete the 12¹/₂" x 12¹/₂" block. Press seams toward the strips.

POSIES ROUND THE SQUARE

Cutting
Cream/white print:
　One template D piece
　Two 6⁷/₈" squares, then cut each square in
　　half once diagonally to make four triangles
Dark blue print:
　Four template C pieces
Red solid:
　Appliqué pieces as per instructions
Medium brown print:
　Appliqué pieces as per instructions

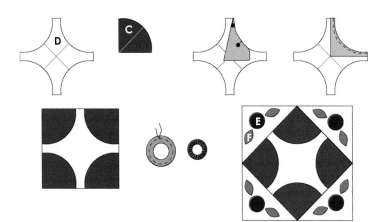

1. Fold the cream/white D piece in half twice diagonally. Finger-press to mark the center on each side. Fold each dark blue C piece in half. Finger press the fold to mark the center.

2. Place a C piece right sides together with one curved part of the D piece, matching the folded creases. Place a pin at the center to hold the pieces in place. Pin the outer edges of the C piece to the outer edges of the D piece. Sew in place, carefully easing the C piece along the edge of the D piece. Repeat to sew the remaining C pieces to the D piece. Press seams toward the C pieces.

3. Sew a cream/white triangle to each side of the center square. Press seams toward the triangles.

4. Prepare card-stock patterns for the E circle and F leaf pieces using patterns given in the pull-out pattern section. Trace four circle patterns on the wrong side of the red solid, adding a ¹/₄" seam allowance around the outside. Cut out. Repeat to

trace and cut out eight leaf pieces from medium brown dot.

5. Thread a needle with one strand of red thread. Knot one end. Carefully stitch gathering stitches around the outer edge of a flower circle about ¹/₈" from the edge. Slip the cardstock circle in the center. Pull the gathering stitches until the fabric is pulled snug around the card stock. Press with steam. Pop out the card-stock circle. Repeat to make four flower circles.

6. Pin a flower circle on the center of each corner. Stitch tiny slip stitches around the outer edge of the circle, catching only one thread on the outer edge of the flower circle to connect the flower to the background.

7. Repeat steps 5 and 6 to make and attach the leaves on each side of the flowers to complete the 12¹/₂" x 12¹/₂" block.

FLYING GEESE

Cutting
Cream/white prints:
　One 6⁷/₈" x 6⁷/₈" square
　Four 3⁷/₈" x 3⁷/₈" squares
Medium blue print:
　One 6⁷/₈" x 6⁷/₈" square
Red dot:
Four 3⁷/₈" x 3⁷/₈" squares

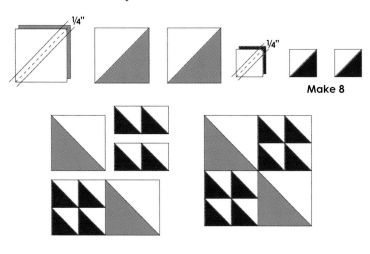

Make 8

1. Draw a diagonal line across the wrong side of the 6⁷/₈" cream/white square and the 3⁷/₈" cream/white squares.

2. Place marked 6⁷/₈" square right sides together on the 6⁷/₈" medium blue square. Sew a ¹/₄" seam on each side of the marked line. Cut apart on the marked line. Open and press toward the blue side to complete two blue units. Repeat with the marked 3⁷/₈" squares and the 3⁷/₈" red squares to make eight red units.

3. Sew four red units together to make a corner unit. Press seams to the red sides Press seams to the red sides. Repeat to make a second corner unit. Sew a corner unit to a blue unit. Press seam toward the blue unit. Repeat. Join the two pieced sections to complete the 12¹/₂" x 12¹/₂" block.

DOUBLE HEART BLOCK

Cutting
Cream/white print:
   One 12¹/₂" x 12¹/₂" square
Red dot, tan print, medium blue print, pink print, dark blue print and multicolor print:
   Appliqué pieces as per instructions

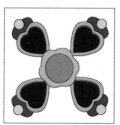

1. Fold the 12¹/₂" square diagonally twice and press to mark appliqué placement lines.
2. Prepare large heart, small heart, flower, flower center, crown circle, and crown pieces using the patterns given in the pull-out pattern section, referring to Fusible Appliqué on page 92.
3. Arrange the appliqué pieces on the creased placement lines. Fuse in place.
4. Using a decorative stitch and thread to match fabrics, stitch around the pieces to complete the 12¹/₂" x 12¹/₂" block.

CHIMNEYS & CORNER STONES

Cutting
Red dot:
   One 3¹/₂" x 3¹/₂" square
   Twelve 2" x 2" squares
Multicolor print:
   Four 2" x 3¹/₂" strips
Medium blue print:
   Four 2" x 6¹/₂" strips
Cream/white print:
   Four 2" x 9¹/₂" strips

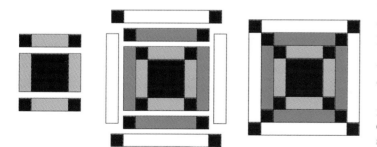

1. Sew the 2" red dot squares to the ends of two 2" x 3¹/₂" multicolor strips, 2" x 6¹/₂" medium blue strips and 2" x 9 1/2" cream/white strips. Press seams toward the strips.
2. Sew the remaining 2" x 3¹/₂" strips to two opposite sides of the 3¹/₂" red square. Press seams toward the strips. Add the pieced multi-color/red strip to the remaining sides. Press seams toward the strips.

3. Repeat step 2 with the 2" x 6¹/₂" medium blue strips and pieced medium blue strips. Repeat step 2 with the 2" x 9¹/₂" cream/white strips and pieced cream/white strips to complete the 12¹/₂" x 12¹/₂" block.

LEMOYNE STAR

Cutting
Medium brown dot:
   Four 4" x 4" squares
Cream/white print:
   One 6¹/₄" x 6¹/₄" square
Tan print:
   Two 2" x 42" strips
Medium blue print:
   Two 2" x 42" strips

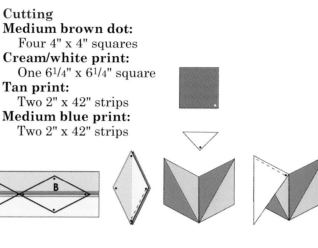

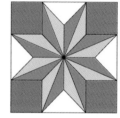

1. Sew a 2" x 42" tan strip lengthwise to a 2" x 42" medium blue strip to make a strip set. Make a second strip set. Press seams open. Apply a heavy coat of spray starch and press dry. Place one strip set wrong side up. Place the B diamond template on the strip set with the centerline on the template matched to the seam of the strip set. Trace around the template with a fine-point pencil. Make a mark through the hole in the template on the seam line at each corner.
2. Continue to mark a total of eight B pieces on the strip sets. Carefully cut out each piece exactly on the marked lines.
3. Place two B pieces right sides together, matching blue to cream/white and aligning the corner dots. Sew from the marked dot at the inside corner to the marked dot at the center corner, locking stitches at each dot. Repeat with remaining B pieces to complete four B units. Press seams to the blue sides.
4. Apply a heavy coat of spray starch to the 6¹/₄" cream/white square. Cut the square twice diagonally to make four triangles.
5. Mark the seam allowance at the inside corner on the wrong side of each triangle. Mark the 1/4" seam allowance at one corner of each 4" medium brown square.

6. Place a triangle right sides together along one edge of a B unit, matching the dot on the triangle to the dot on the B unit. Pin to hold the pieces together. Stitch from the dot to the outside edge. Repeat to stitch the triangle to the other edge of the B unit. Press seams toward the B unit. Repeat with each B unit.

7. Repeat step 3 to sew two B units together. Repeat. Sew the two sections together to complete the star unit.

8. Repeat step 6 to sew a 4" medium brown square between the remaining star points to complete the 12¹/₂" x 12¹/₂" block. Press seams toward the B units.

OHIO STAR

Cutting
Cream/white print:
  Four 4¹/₂" x 4¹/₂" squares
  Two 5¹/₄" x 5¹/₄" squares
Multicolor print:
  One 4¹/₂" x 4¹/₂" square
Dark blue print:
  Two 5¹/₄" x 5¹/₄" squares

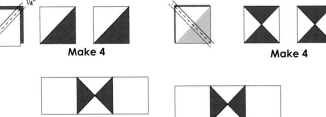

Make 4   Make 4

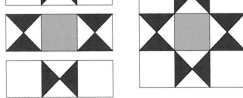

1. Draw a diagonal line across the wrong side of the 5¹/₄" cream/white squares.

2. Place a marked square right sides together with a 5¹/₄" dark blue square. Sew a ¹/₄" on each side of the marked line. Cut apart on the marked line. Open and press toward the blue side. Repeat with the remaining 5¹/₄" squares to make a total of four cream/blue units.

3. Place two cream/blue units right sides together with opposite fabrics touching. Draw a diagonal line across the stitched seam on the top unit. Sew a ¹/₄" seam on each side of the marked line. Cut apart on the marked line. Open and press to complete two side units. Repeat with the remaining cream/blue units to make a total of four side units.

4. Sew the 4¹/₂" multicolor square between two side units to make the center row. Press seams toward the square. Sew a side unit between two 4¹/₂" cream/white squares to make a side row. Press seams toward the squares. Repeat to make

a second side row. Sew the center row between the side rows to complete the 12¹/₂" x 12¹/₂" block. Press seam toward the center row.

BACHELOR'S PUZZLE

Cutting
Tan print:
  One 6¹/₂" x 6¹/₂" square
Medium blue print:
  Four 3¹/₂" x 3¹/₂" squares
  Two 3⁷/₈" x 3⁷/₈" squares
Medium brown dot:
  Four 3⁷/₈" x 3⁷/₈" squares
Cream/white print:
  Two 3⁷/₈" x 3⁷/₈" squares
Red dot:
  Four 3¹/₂" x 3¹/₂" squares

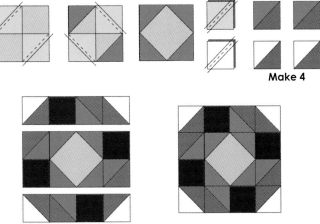

Make 4

Make 4

1. Draw a diagonal line across the wrong side of the 3¹/₂" medium blue squares, the 3⁷/₈" medium blue squares and the 3⁷/₈" cream/white squares.

2. Place a marked 3¹/₂" square right sides together on opposite corners of the 6¹/₂" tan square. Sew on the marked lines. Trim, leaving a ¹/₄" seam allowance. Open and press toward the blue corners. Repeat on the remaining corners of the tan square to complete the center unit.

3. Place the marked 3⁷/₈" medium blue squares right sides together on two 3⁷/₈" medium brown squares. Sew ¹/₄" on each side of the marked lines. Cut apart on the marked lines. Open and press toward the blue sides to make four blue/brown units. Repeat with the marked 3⁷/₈" cream/white squares and the remaining 3⁷/₈" medium brown squares to make four cream/brown units.

4. Sew a blue/brown unit to a 3¹/₂" red square to make a side unit. Press seam toward the red square. Repeat to make four side units.

5. Sew a side unit to two opposite sides of the center unit to make the center row. Press seams toward the side units. Sew a side unit between two cream/brown units to make a side row. Press seams toward the side unit. Repeat to make a second side row. Sew the center row between the side rows to complete the 12¹/₂" x 12¹/₂" block. Press seams toward the side rows.

QUILT ASSEMBLY AND FINISHING
Note: Refer to the Assembly Diagram throughout the following steps. Press seams toward each border strip as added.

1. Lay out the blocks in four rows with three blocks in each row.

2. Sew the blocks in one row together with four 2¹/₂" x 12¹/₂" medium brown print strips. Press seams toward the strips. Repeat to complete the four block rows.

3. Sew three 2¹/₂" x 12¹/₂" medium brown print strips together with four 2¹/₂" red solid squares to make a sashing row. Press seams toward the strips. Repeat to complete a total of five sashing rows.

4. Sew the block rows alternately together with the sashing rows to complete the 44¹/₂" x 58¹/₂" quilt center. Press seams toward the sashing rows.

5. *First Border.* Sew the 1¹/₂" x 42" dark blue print strips short ends together to make a long strip. Cut into two 58¹/₂" strips and two 46¹/₂" strips. Sew the longer strips to the long sides and the shorter strips to the top and bottom of the quilt center.

6. *Second Border.* Sew the 6¹/₂" x 42" blue stripe strips short ends together to make a long strip. Cut into two 60¹/₂" strips and two 46¹/₂" strips. Sew the longer strips to the long sides. Sew a 6¹/₂" medium brown print square to each end of the 46¹/₂" strips. Press seams toward the strips. Sew these strips to the top and bottom of the quilt center.

7. *Third Border.* Sew the 2¹/₂" x 42" dark blue print strips short ends together to make a long strip. Cut into two 72¹/₂" strips and two 62¹/₂" strips. Sew the longer strips to the long sides and the shorter strips to the top and bottom of the quilt center to complete the top.

8. Layer, quilt and bind the quilt using the seven 2¹/₂" x 42" dark blue print binding strips, referring to the Finishing Basics on page 93.

Assembly Diagram

Chapter 6

The Dakota Room

Each room or area of the Village is filled with a variety of items that fit a certain theme. The Dakota Room holds bed quilts, wall quilts, table toppers and pillows that feature the many motifs of our area. The most well-known attraction in the area is Mt. Rushmore, but there are so many different things to see and enjoy here. I have tried to fill this room with projects that highlight this part of our wonderful country. The Black Hills area is known for its beauty and many of its animals. The buffalo reigns in this region and is a very popular motif for the quilters who visit the shop. Two of our best selling quilts feature the buffalo. The quilt project in this chapter is My Heart is in the Hills.

Rapid City has also been advertised as the Star of the West, so a small quilt featuring western fabrics and the easy to make Sawtooth Star Block is included in this chapter. Every little cowboy or cowgirl would enjoy cuddling up in this simple to make quilt.

My Heart is in The Hills

This quilt was designed as a local Shop Hop quilt. The easy half-square triangle unit is used to make the entire quilt. Simple fabric prints and colors were used to create the base of the quilt to make a perfect background for the fusible appliqué.

Skill Level: Beginner
Finished quilt size: 32" x 38"
Block size sewn into quilt: 3" x 3"
Number of blocks: 4

SUPPLIES

Yardage is based on 42"-wide cotton fabric.
- Scrap of tan print
- $1/8$ yard brown print
- $1/8$ yard dark brown print
- $1/8$ yard gold/brown print
- $1/4$ yard medium green print
- $1/4$ yard dark green/yellow print
- $1/4$ yard cloud print
- $1/4$ yard dark blue print
- $1/4$ yard very dark green print
- $1/4$ yard light green print
- $1/4$ yard green/brown print
- $1/4$ yard medium blue print
- $1/4$ yard cream/tan print
- $1/3$ yard gold print
- $7/8$ yard dark green plaid
- 40" x 46" piece of backing
- 40" x 46" piece of batting
- Thread to match fabrics
- 1 yard fusible web
- Rotary cutter, ruler and mat
- Basic sewing supplies

CUTTING INSTRUCTIONS:

From the tan print, brown print, dark brown print, gold/brown print, medium green print and dark green/yellow print, cut:
Appliqué pieces as per instructions

From the cloud print, cut:
Two $6^7/8$" x $6^7/8$" squares

From the dark blue print, cut:
Four $6^7/8$" x $6^7/8$" squares

From the very dark green print, cut:
Two $6^7/8$" x $6^7/8$" squares

From the light green print, cut:
Four $6^7/8$" x $6^7/8$" squares

From the green/brown print, cut:
Three $6^7/8$" x $6^7/8$" squares

From the medium blue print, cut:
One $6^7/8$" x $6^7/8$" square

From the cream/tan print, cut:
One $6^7/8$" x 42" strip; recut into two $6^7/8$" squares, two $6^1/2$" squares, eight $1^7/8$" squares and four $1^1/2$" squares

From the gold print, cut:
Two $1^1/2$" x $30^1/2$" strips (border)
Two $1^1/2$" x $26^1/2$" strips (border)
One $2^1/2$" x 42" strip; recut into four $2^1/2$" squares and eight $1^7/8$" squares

From the dark green plaid, cut:
Two $3^1/2$" x $32^1/2$" strips (border)
Two $3^1/2$" x $26^1/2$" strips (border)
Four $2^1/2$" x 42" strips (binding)

INSTRUCTIONS

Note: Use a $1/4$" seam allowance throughout. Sew all pieces with right sides together and edges aligned. Press seams toward the darker fabric after adding each piece.

Bear Paw Blocks

1. Draw a diagonal line across the wrong side of the $1^7/8$" cream/tan squares.

2. Place a marked square right sides together on a $1^7/8$" gold print square. Sew a $1/4$" seam on each side of the marked line. Cut apart on the line. Open and press toward the gold side to complete two triangle units. Repeat with all $1^7/8$" cream/tan and gold squares to make a total of sixteen triangle units.

Make 16

3. Sew two triangle units together to make a strip. Press seam to the gold side. Repeat to make a total of four strips and four reverse strips.

Make 4   Make 4
Reversed

4. Sew a triangle strip to one side of a 2½" gold print square. Press seam toward the square. Sew a reverse triangle strip to one side of a 1½" cream/tan square. Press seam toward the square. Join the two pieced units to complete one 3½" x 3½" block. Repeat to make a total of four blocks.

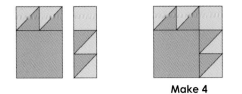

Make 4

Landscape Units

1. Draw a diagonal line across the wrong side of the 6⅞" cloud print, very dark green print, green/brown print and cream/tan print squares.

2. Place a marked cloud print square right sides together with a 6⅞" dark blue print square. Sew a ¼" seam on each side of the marked line. Cut apart on the line. Open and press toward the dark blue side to complete two A units. Repeat to make a total of four A units.

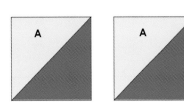

Make 4

3. Repeat with two marked very dark green squares and two dark blue squares to make four B units.

Make 4

4. Repeat step two with a marked green/brown square and the medium blue square to make two C units.

Make 2

5. Repeat with two marked green/brown squares and two light green squares to make four D units.

Make 4

6. Repeat with two marked cream/tan squares and two light green squares to make four E units.

Make 4

QUILT ASSEMBLY AND FINISHING

Note: Refer to the Assembly Diagram throughout the following steps. Press seams toward each border strip as added.

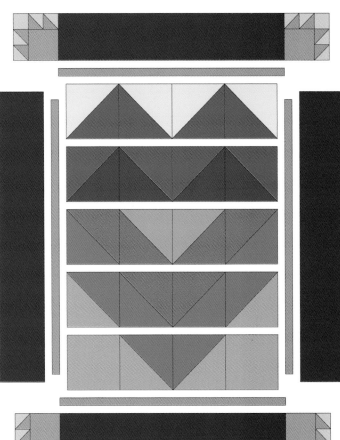

Assembly Diagram

1. Sew the four A units together to make row 1. Press seams to the left.

2. Sew the four B units together to make row 2. Press seams to the right.

3. Sew two C and two D units together to make row 3. Press seams to the left.

4. Sew two D units and two E units together to make row 4. Press seams to the right.

5. Sew two E units and two 6½" cream/tan squares together to make row 5. Press seams to the left.

6. Sew the rows together to complete the 24½" x 30½" quilt center.

7. *Inner Border* Sew the $1^{1}/_{2}$" x $30^{1}/_{2}$" gold print strips to the long sides and the $1^{1}/_{2}$" x $26^{1}/_{2}$" gold print strips to the top and bottom of the quilt center.

8. *Outer Border* Sew the $3^{1}/_{2}$" x $32^{1}/_{2}$" dark green plaid strips to the long sides. Sew a Bear Paw block to each end of the $3^{1}/_{2}$" x $26^{1}/_{2}$" dark green plaid strips referring to the Assembly Diagram for positioning of the blocks. Press seams toward the strips. Sew these strips to the top and bottom of the quilt center to complete the top.

9. Referring to the basic instructions for Fusible Appliqué on page 92, prepare appliqué pieces for the trees, grass and buffalo using the patterns given in the pull-out pattern section.

10. Arrange the large tree pieces on the quilt center in numerical order referring to the quilt photo for positioning suggestions. Arrange the remaining appliqué pieces on the quilt center. Fuse pieces in place.

11. Sew around each shape using a decorative stitch and matching thread.

12. Layer, quilt and bind the edges using the four $2^{1}/_{2}$" x 42" dark green binding strips, referring to the Finishing Basics on page 93.

Star of the West Quilt

This quilt is made with a western-themed fabric. The bright prints used in the blocks become the focus of the design. Easy-to-make basic blocks make this quilt shine.

Skill Level: Beginner
Finished quilt size: 54" x 54"
Block size sewn into quilt: 8" x 8" and 6" x 6"
Number of blocks: 16 and 4

SUPPLIES

Yardage is based on 42"-wide cotton fabric.
- One fat eighth of eight different western prints
- One fat quarter each gold, blue, red and black star prints
- 1/8 yard dark blue print
- 3/4 yard light blue marble
- 1 1/4 yards cream print
- 1 1/2 yards red print
- 62" x 62" piece of backing fabric
- 62" x 62" piece of batting
- Thread in colors to match fabrics
- Rotary cutter, ruler and mat
- Basic sewing supplies

CUTTING INSTRUCTIONS

From each of the western prints, cut:
One 8 1/2" x 8 1/2" square

From each of the star prints, cut:
Two 2 1/2" x 21" strips; recut into sixteen 2 1/2" squares
One 4 1/2" x 21" strip; recut into two 4 1/2" squares and one 3 1/2" square
One 2" x 21" strip; recut into eight 2" squares

From the dark blue print, cut:
One 2 1/2" x 42" strip; recut into nine 2 1/2" squares

From the light blue marble, cut:
Six 2 1/2" x 42" strips; recut into twenty-four 2 1/2" x 8 1/2" strips
Four 2 1/2" x 42" strips (border)

From the cream print, cut:
Six 2 1/2" x 42" strips; recut into thirty-two 2 1/2" squares and thirty-two 2 1/2" x 4 1/2" rectangles
Four 4 1/2" x 42" strips; recut into thirty-two 4 1/2" squares
Three 2" x 42" strips; recut into sixteen 2" squares and sixteen 2" x 3 1/2" rectangles

From the red print, cut:
Five 6 1/2" x 42" strips (border)
Six 2 1/2" x 42" strips (binding)

INSTRUCTIONS

Note: Use a 1/4" seam allowance throughout. Sew all pieces with right sides together and edges aligned. Press seams toward the darker fabric after adding each piece or as indicated.

Square-in-a-Square Blocks
1. Draw a diagonal line across the wrong side of the 4 1/2" cream print squares.
2. Place a marked cream square right sides together on one corner of one 8 1/2" western print square. Sew on the marked line. Trim seam allowance to 1/4". Open and press toward the western square. Repeat on the remaining corners of the square to complete one 8 1/2" x 8 1/2" block.

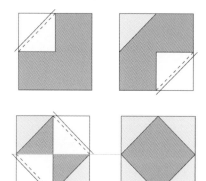

Make 8

3. Repeat with each 8 1/2" western square to complete a total of eight Square-in-a-Square blocks.

Star Blocks
1. Draw a diagonal line across the wrong side of the 2 1/2" and 2" star print squares.
2. Place a marked 2 1/2" square right sides together on one end of a 2 1/2" x 4 1/2" cream rectangle. Sew on the marked line. Trim leaving a 1/4" seam allowance. Open and press toward the star print. Repeat with a matching 2 1/2" square on the remaining end of the rectangle to complete one point unit. Repeat to make a total of four matching point units.

Make 4

3. Sew a point unit to two opposite sides of a matching 4½" star print square to make the center row. Press seams toward the square.

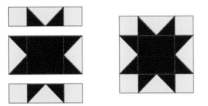

4. Sew a 2½" cream square to each end of the remaining point units to make two side rows. Press seams toward the squares.

5. Sew the center row between the side rows to complete one 8½" x 8½" large star block. Press seams toward the center row.

6. Repeat steps 2–5 to complete a total of eight large star blocks.

7. Repeat steps 2–5 with the 2" marked star print squares, 3½" star print squares, 2" x 3½" cream rectangles and 2" cream squares to make four 6½" x 6½" small star blocks.

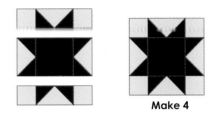

Make 4

QUILT ASSEMBLY AND FINISHING

Note: Refer to the Assembly Diagram throughout the following steps. Press seams toward each border strip as added.

1. Sew two large Star blocks and two Square-in-a-Square blocks alternately together with three 2½" x 8½" light blue marble strips to make a block row. Press seams toward the blue marble strips. Repeat to make 3 more block rows, referring to the Assembly Diagram for positioning of the blocks.

Assembly Diagram

2. Sew four 2¹/2" x 8¹/2" light blue marble strips alternately together with three 2¹/2" dark blue print squares to make a sashing row. Press seams toward the strips. Repeat to make a total of three sashing rows.

3. Sew the block rows alternately together with the sashing rows to complete the 38¹/2" x 38¹/2" quilt center. Press seams toward the sashing rows.

4. *Inner Border* Sew the four 2¹/2" x 42" light blue marble strips short ends together to make a long strip. Cut into two 38¹/2" lengths and two 42¹/2" lengths. Sew the shorter strips to two oppo-

site sides and the longer strips to the remaining sides of the quilt center.

5. *Outer Border* Sew the five 6¹/2" x 42" red print strips short ends together to make a long strip. Cut into four 42¹/2" lengths. Sew a strip to two opposite sides of the quilt center. Sew a small Star block to each end of the remaining strips. Press seams toward the strips. Sew these strips to the remaining sides of the quilt center to complete the top.

6. Layer, quilt and bind the edges using the six 2¹/2" x 42" red print binding strips, referring to the Finishing Basics on page 93.

Chapter 7

The Kids' Cozy Company

Walk into this room and visions of childhood teddy bears, bunnies, and fresh fabric quilts, pillows, wall quilts, and table toppers surround you. This is the room our bear collectors and Sun Bonnet Sue collectors love to visit.

Many of the items in this room are created by our consignors. The fun colorful fabrics used to make the various quilts, pillows and wall quilts provide a vintage touch. The bunnies and bears add that warm cozy feeling that we all love.

The projects in this chapter are made from coordinates of a paper doll collection. The wonderful bright pink, yellow and green simply make the bed area sing. I have used the very simple spool block design and a fun flower appliqué to make this bedroom collection.

Spoolin' Around Quilt

New vibrant prints make the traditional Spool block pop when sewn on-point to make this quick quilt. The smaller Spool blocks in the border are placed to make a completely different design than that of the center.

Skill Level: Beginner
Finished quilt size: 70" x 100"
Block sizes sewn into quilt: 9" x 9" and 6" x 6"
Number of blocks: 23 and 46

SUPPLIES

Yardage is based on 42"-wide cotton fabric.
- $1^1/2$ yards green print
- $2^1/4$ yards yellow weave print
- $3^1/8$ yards pink/yellow floral
- $3^1/3$ yards lavender dot
- 78" x 108" piece of backing fabric
- 78" x 108" piece of batting
- Thread in colors to match fabrics
- Rotary cutter, ruler and mat
- Basic sewing supplies

CUTTING INSTRUCTIONS

From the green print, cut:
Twelve $1^1/2$" x 42" strips (borders)
One $6^1/2$" x 42" strip; recut into four $6^1/2$" squares (border)
Nine $2^1/2$" x 42" strips (binding)

From the yellow weave print, cut:
Fifteen $1^1/2$" x 42" strips, recut into sixty $1^1/2$" x $9^1/2$" strips
Four $1^1/2$" x 42" strips (border)
Seventeen $2^1/2$" x 42" strips (borders)

From the pink/yellow floral, cut:
Fourteen $3^1/2$" x 42" strips; recut into twenty-three $3^1/2$" x $9^1/2$" rectangles and ninety-two $3^1/2$" squares
Twenty $2^1/2$" x 42" strips; recut into forty-six $2^1/2$" x $6^1/2$" rectangles and one hundred eighty-four $2^1/2$" squares
Two $1^1/2$" x 42" strips; recut into thirty-eight $1^1/2$" squares

From the lavender dot, cut:
Sixteen $2^1/2$" x 42" strips; recut into ninety-two $2^1/2$" x $6^1/2$" rectangles
Twelve $3^1/2$" x 42" strips, recut into forty-six $3^1/2$" x 9 1/2" rectangles
Two $15^3/8$" x 42" strips, recut into three $15^3/8$" squares and two $8^5/8$" squares. Cut the $15^3/8$" squares twice diagonally to make twelve setting triangles and the $8^5/8$" squares in half once diagonally to make four corner triangles

INSTRUCTIONS

Note: Use a $1/4$" seam allowance throughout. Sew all pieces with right sides together and edges aligned. Press seams toward the darker fabric after adding each piece or as indicated.

Spool Blocks
1. Draw a diagonal line across the wrong side of the $3^1/2$" and $2^1/2$" pink/yellow floral squares.
2. Place a marked $3^1/2$" square right sides together on each end of the $3^1/2$" x $9^1/2$" lavender dot rectangles. Sew on the marked lines. Trim seam allowances to $1/4$", open and press toward the floral corners to complete 46 large side units.

Make 46

3. Sew a $3^1/2$" x $9^1/2$" pink/yellow floral rectangle lengthwise between two large side units to complete one $9^1/2$" x $9^1/2$" large Spool block. Press seams toward the floral rectangle. Repeat to make a total of 23 blocks.

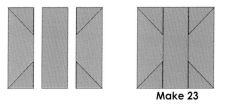

Make 23

4. Repeat step 2 with the marked $2^1/2$" squares and the $2^1/2$" x $6^1/2$" lavender dot rectangles to make 92 small side units.

Make 92

5. Repeat step 3 with the $2^1/2$" x $6^1/2$" pink/yellow floral rectangles and the small side units to make forty-six $6^1/2$" x $6^1/2$" small Spool blocks.

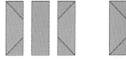

Make 46

QUILT ASSEMBLY AND FINISHING

Note: Refer to the Assembly Diagram throughout the following steps. Press seams toward each border strip as added.

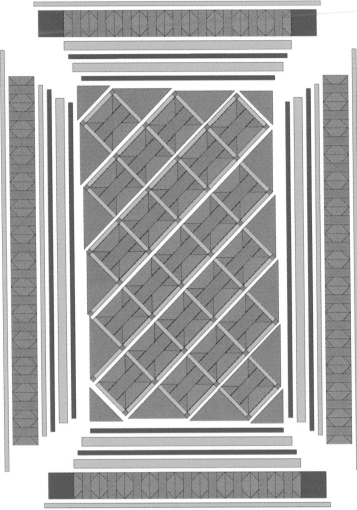

Assembly Diagram

1. Sew the large Spool blocks together with 1$^{1/2}$" x 9$^{1/2}$" yellow weave print strips to make block rows. Press seams toward the yellow strips.

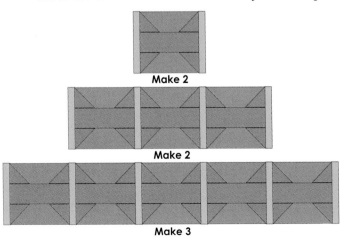

Make 2

Make 2

Make 3

2. Sew the 1$^{1/2}$" pink/yellow floral squares together with the 1$^{1/2}$" x 9$^{1/2}$" yellow weave strips to make sashing rows. Press seams toward the yellow strips.

3. Sew the block rows together with the sashing rows and the lavender dot setting triangles. Press seams toward the sashing rows and side triangles. Add a lavender dot corner triangle to complete the 44$^{1/2}$" x 72$^{1/2}$" quilt center.

4. *First Border.* Sew the 1$^{1/2}$" x 42" green print strips short ends together to make a long strip. Cut into two 72$^{1/2}$" strips, two 46$^{1/2}$" strips, two 78$^{1/2}$" strips and two 52$^{1/2}$" strips. Sew the 72$^{1/2}$" strips to the long sides and the 46$^{1/2}$" strips to the top and bottom of the quilt center. Set aside the 78$^{1/2}$" and 52$^{1/2}$" strips for the third border.

5. *Second Border.* Sew the 2$^{1/2}$" x 42" yellow weave strips short ends together to make a long strip. Cut into two 74$^{1/2}$" strips, two 50$^{1/2}$" strips, two 54$^{1/2}$" strips, two 96$^{1/2}$" strips and two 70$^{1/2}$" strips. Sew the 74$^{1/2}$" strips to the long sides and the 50$^{1/2}$" strips to the top and bottom of the quilt center. Set aside the 54$^{1/2}$" strips for the fourth border and the 96$^{1/2}$" and 70$^{1/2}$" strips for the sixth border.

6. *Third Border.* Sew the 78$^{1/2}$" green strips from step 4 to the long sides and the 52$^{1/2}$" green strips from step 4 to the top and bottom of the quilt center.

7. *Fourth Border.* Sew the four 1$^{1/2}$" x 42" yellow weave strips short ends together to make a long strip. Cut into two 80$^{1/2}$" strips. Sew these strips to the long sides of the quilt center and the 2$^{1/2}$" x 54$^{1/2}$" yellow strips from step 5 to the top and bottom.

8. *Fifth Pieced Border.* Sew 14 small Spool blocks together to make a side strip. Press seams in one direction. Repeat to make a second side strip. Sew a strip to the long sides of the quilt center. Press seams back toward the yellow borders. Sew nine small Spool blocks together to make the top strip. Repeat to make the bottom strip. Sew a 6$^{1/2}$" green print square to each end of the top and bottom strips. Press seams toward the squares. Sew these strips to the top and bottom of the quilt center. Press seams back toward the yellow borders.

9. *Sixth Border.* Sew the 96$^{1/2}$" yellow strips from step 5 to the long sides and the 70$^{1/2}$" yellow strips from step 5 to the top and bottom of the quilt center to complete the top.

10. Layer, quilt and bind the quilt using the nine 2$^{1/2}$" x 42" green print binding strips, referring to the Finishing Basics on page 93.

Make 2

Make 2

Make 2

Make 2

Spoolin' Bouquet Wall Quilt

Use one Spool block to make the "vase" that holds the large machine appliquéd bouquet.
This wall quilt looks very nice when placed above the bed.

Skill Level: Beginner
Finished quilt size: 19" x 35"
Block size sewn into quilt: 9" x 9"
Number of blocks: 1

SUPPLIES

Yardage is based on 42"-wide cotton fabric.
- Fat eighth lavender dot
- Fat eighth pink/yellow floral
- 3/8 yard yellow weave print
- 1/2 yard cream print
- 3/4 yard green print
- 27" x 43" piece of backing fabric
- 27" x 43" piece of batting
- Thread in colors to match fabrics
- 3/4 yard fusible web
- Rotary cutter, ruler and mat
- Basic sewing supplies

CUTTING INSTRUCTIONS

From the lavender dot, cut:
One 3$\frac{1}{2}$" x 21" strip; recut into two 3$\frac{1}{2}$" x 9$\frac{1}{2}$"
    rectangles

From the pink/yellow floral, cut:
Appliqué pieces as per instructions

From the yellow weave print, cut:
Three 2$\frac{1}{2}$" x 42" strips; recut into two 2$\frac{1}{2}$" x 31$\frac{1}{2}$"
    strips and two 2$\frac{1}{2}$" x 19$\frac{1}{2}$" strips (border)
Appliqué pieces as per instructions

From the cream print, cut:
One 13$\frac{1}{2}$"x 42" strip; recut into one 13$\frac{1}{2}$" x 20$\frac{1}{2}$"
    rectangle, six 3$\frac{1}{2}$" squares and two 2$\frac{1}{2}$" x 9$\frac{1}{2}$"
    strips

From the green print, cut:
One 3$\frac{1}{2}$" x 42" strip; recut into one 3$\frac{1}{2}$" square
Three 1$\frac{1}{2}$" x 42" strips; recut into two 1$\frac{1}{2}$" x 29$\frac{1}{2}$"
    strips and two 1$\frac{1}{2}$" x 15$\frac{1}{2}$" strips (border)
Three 2$\frac{1}{2}$" x 42" strips (binding)
Appliqué pieces as per instructions

INSTRUCTIONS

Note: Use a 1/4" seam allowance throughout. Sew all pieces with right sides together and edges aligned. Press seams toward the darker fabric after adding each piece or as indicated.

Flower Panel

Note: Refer to Fusible Appliqué on page 92 to prepare the flower panel.

1. Prepare fusible appliqué pieces for the flowers, centers, leaves and stems using the patterns given in the pull-out pattern section.
2. Fuse the appliqué pieces on the 13$\frac{1}{2}$" x 20$\frac{1}{2}$" cream print rectangle referring to the project photo when placing the pieces.
3. Stitch the pieces in place with a decorative stitch and thread to match fabrics.

Spool Block

1. Draw a diagonal line across the wrong side of four 3$\frac{1}{2}$" cream print squares.
2. Place a marked square right sides together on each end of the 3$\frac{1}{2}$" x 9$\frac{1}{2}$" lavender dot rectangles. Sew on the marked lines. Trim seam allowances to 1/4", open and press toward the cream corners to complete two end units.

Make 2

3. Sew the 3$\frac{1}{2}$" green print square between two 3$\frac{1}{2}$" cream print squares to make the center unit.

4. Sew the center unit lengthwise between the end units to complete the 9$\frac{1}{2}$" x 9$\frac{1}{2}$" Spool block. Press seams toward the center row.

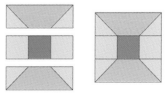

QUILT ASSEMBLY AND FINISHING

Note: Refer to the Assembly Diagram throughout the following steps. Press seams toward each border strip as added.

1. Sew a 2 1/2" x 9 1/2" cream print rectangle to opposite sides of the Spool block. Press seams toward the rectangles.

2. Sew the flower panel to the top of the Spool block section to complete the quilt center. Press seam toward the Spool block section.

3. *Inner Border.* Sew the 1 1/2" x 29 1/2" green print strips to the long sides and the 1 1/2" x 15 1/2" strips to the top and bottom of the quilt center.

4. *Outer Border.* Sew the 2 1/2" x 31 1/2" yellow weave strips to the long sides and the 2 1/2" x 19 1/2" strips to the top and bottom to complete the top.

5. Layer, quilt and bind using the three 2 1/2" x 42" green print strips, referring to Finishing Basics on page 93.

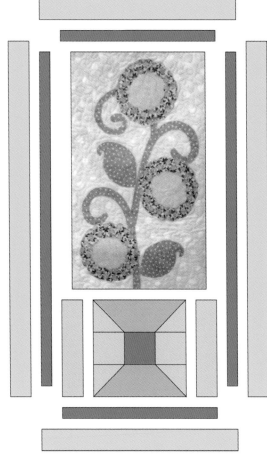

Assembly Diagram

Village Gatherings

Giving back to the community is a very important part of this business. The Thimble Cottage Quilt Village has been the meeting place for customer quilt clubs, book clubs and bible study groups. The kitchen area has held baby showers, wedding showers, birthday parties and family holiday gatherings. We offer the kitchen area to local groups at no charge for their gatherings. The good will this creates and word-of-mouth advertising from these events are very valuable to the business.

I have been the design coordinator for our local Festival of Trees for the past 12 years. This event is the highlight of the holiday season and provides much needed services to local patients.

Most recently our customers were challenged to make pillowcases from their stash. More than 50 pillowcases were made and donated. I provided pillows to fill the cases. They were delivered to a local charity.

Chapter 8

The Hot Chocolate Club

Step into the Hot Chocolate Club and you will smile from ear to ear. Years ago I started the Hot Chocolate Club and invited our customers to join us in making a Snowman Block of the Month. We started with the Blizzard Bunch Block of the Month. Oh what fun! I realized that Snowmen make people smile and I knew I had to design more. I have designed a snowman, snow woman, or snow babies pattern every year for more than 10 years and I don't think there is an end to these wonderful characters.

One of the most popular quilts that I have ever designed was called Through the Winter Window. This wall quilt made the cover of *The Quilter* magazine and it was a huge success. To this day I have quilters wanting me to design a new quilt using snowmen and a window theme.

Every corner of the Hot Chocolate Club is filled from the ceiling to the floor with designs that never grow old or boring. Come on in and enjoy! Perhaps you would like to make the collection of snowmen projects featured in this chapter. But be careful—you may find them just as addictive as my customers have!

Snow Globe Wall Quilt

This cute snowman wall quilt is sure to please. Each pieced "tummy" adds a bit of interest to this fun project. These snowmen will have you smiling all winter long.

Skill Level: Beginner
Finished quilt size: 34" x 34"
Block sizes sewn into quilt: 12" x 12", 6" x 12" and 6" x 6"
Number of blocks: 1, 4 and 4

SUPPLIES

Yardage is based on 42"-wide cotton fabric.
- 2" x 6" piece black print
- 3" x 6" piece orange print
- 1/3 yard total red prints
- 3/8 yard total cream/white prints
- 5/8 yard gold print
- 5/8 yard green print
- 2/3 yard dark blue plaid
- 2/3 yard total dark blue prints
- 42" x 42" piece of backing fabric
- 42" x 42" piece of batting
- Thread in colors to match fabrics
- Black embroidery floss
- Embroidery needle
- 1/8 yard fusible web
- Rotary cutter, ruler and mat
- Basic sewing supplies

CUTTING INSTRUCTIONS

From the black print and orange print, cut:
Appliqué pieces as per instructions

From the red prints, cut:
One 2 1/2" x 42" strip; recut eight 2 1/2" squares
One 4 1/2" x 42" strip; recut into five 4 1/2" squares

From the cream/white prints, cut:
One 4 1/2" x 42" strip; recut into four 4 1/2" squares, eight 1 1/2" x 4 1/2" rectangles and two 2 7/8" squares
Two 2 1/2" x 42" strips; recut into eight 2 1/2" x 6 1/2" rectangles

From the gold print, cut:
Two 2" x 42" strips; recut into thirty-two 2" squares
One 4 7/8" x 42" strip; recut into one 4 7/8" square, eight 3 1/2" squares and two 2 1/2" x 4 1/2" rectangles
Two 1 1/2" x 24 1/2" strips (border)
Two 1 1/2" x 26 1/2" strips (border)

From the green print, cut:
One 4 7/8" x 42" strip; recut into one 4 7/8" square and four 2 1/2" squares
Four 2 1/2" x 42" strips (binding)

From the dark blue plaid, cut:
Four 4 1/2" x 26 1/2" strips (border)

From the dark blue prints, cut:
Two 1 1/2" x 42" strips; recut into eight 1 1/2" x 4 1/2" rectangles and thirty-two 1 1/2" squares
Two 3 1/2" x 42" strips; recut into eight 3 1/2" squares and four 3 1/2" x 6 1/2" rectangles
One 2 7/8" x 42" strip; recut into two 2 7/8" squares and five 2 1/2" squares
Three 2" x 42" strips; recut into sixteen 2" squares and sixteen 2" x 3 1/2" rectangles

INSTRUCTIONS

Note: Use a 1/4" seam allowance throughout. Sew all pieces with right sides together and edges aligned. Press seams toward the darker fabric after adding each piece or as indicated.

Nine-Patch Star Block

1. Sew a 2 1/2" red print square between two 2 1/2" dark blue print squares to make an end row. Press seams toward the dark blue squares. Repeat to make a second end row. Sew a 2 1/2" dark blue print square between two 2 1/2" red print squares to make the center row. Press seams toward the dark blue square.

Make 2

Make 1

2. Sew the center row between the end rows to complete the block center. Press seams toward the end rows.

3. Draw a diagonal line across the wrong side of the 3 1/2" gold print squares. Place a marked square right sides together on one end of each 3 1/2" x 6 1/2" dark blue print rectangles. Sew on the marked lines. Trim leaving a 1/4" seam allowance. Open and press seam toward the gold corner. Repeat on the remaining end of each rectangle to complete four side units.

Make 4

4. Sew a side unit to two opposite sides of the block center. Press seams toward the block center. Sew a 3¹/2" dark blue print square to each end of the remaining side units. Press seams toward the squares. Sew these strips to the remaining sides of the block center to complete the 12¹/2" x 12¹/2" Nine-Patch Star block. Press seams toward the block center.

Sawtooth Star Blocks

1. Repeat step 3 of the Nine-Patch Star block using the 2" gold print squares and 2" x 3¹/2" dark blue print rectangles to complete 16 side units.

Make 16

2. Sew a side unit to two opposite sides of four 3¹/2" dark blue print squares. Press seams toward the squares to make the center rows. Sew a 2" dark blue print square to each end of the remaining side units. Press seams toward the squares. Sew these strips to opposite sides of the center rows to complete four 6¹/2" x 6¹/2" Sawtooth Star blocks.

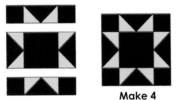

Make 4

Snowman Blocks

1. Draw a diagonal line across the wrong side of the 1¹/2" dark blue print squares.

2. Place a marked square right sides together on the corners of each 4¹/2" cream/white print square. Sew on the marked lines. Trim leaving a ¹/4" seam allowance. Open and press toward the dark blue corners. Sew a 1¹/2" x 4¹/2" dark blue print rectangle to two opposite sides of each square to complete four head units.

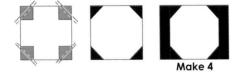

Make 4

3. Repeat step 2 on the ends of the 2¹/2" x 6¹/2" cream/white print rectangles to complete eight shoulder/base units.

Make 8

4. To make the flying-geese tummy, draw a diagonal line across the wrong side of the four remaining 2¹/2" red print squares. Place a marked square right sides together on one end of each 2¹/2" x 4¹/2" gold print rectangle. Sew on the marked lines. Trim leaving a ¹/4" seam allowance. Open and press toward the red corner. Repeat on the remaining end of each rectangle. Sew the two units together to complete the flying-geese tummy.

Make 2

5. To make the square-in-a-square tummy, draw a diagonal line across the wrong side of the four 2¹/2" green print squares. Place a marked square right sides together on two opposite corners of one 4¹/2" red print square. Sew on the marked line. Trim leaving a ¹/4" seam allowance. Open and press toward the green corners. Repeat on the remaining corners to complete the square-in-a-square tummy.

6. To make the pinwheel tummy, draw a diagonal line across the wrong side of the 2⁷/8" cream/white print squares. Place the marked squares right sides together on the 2⁷/8" dark blue print squares. Sew a ¹/4" seam on each side of the marked line. Cut apart on the marked line. Open and press toward the dark blue sides. Sew two triangle units together to make a row. Repeat. Sew the rows together to make the pinwheel tummy.

7. To make the hour-glass tummy, draw a diagonal line across the wrong side of the 4⁷/8" gold print square. Place the marked square right sides together on the 4⁷/8" green print square. Sew a ¹/4" seam on each side of the marked line. Cut apart on the marked line. Open and press toward the green side. Place the triangle units right sides together with opposite fabrics touching. Draw a diagonal line across the seam on the wrong side of the top triangle unit. Sew a ¹/4" seam on each side of the marked line. Cut apart on the marked line. Open and press to make the hour-glass tummy. Set aside the extra unit for another project or discard it.

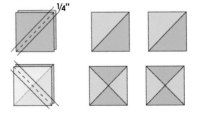

8. Sew a 1¹/2" x 4¹/2" cream/white print rectangle to two opposite sides of each tummy. Press seams toward the rectangles. Sew a shoulder/base unit to the top and bottom of each

Instructions continued on page 82

tummy to complete four body units. Press seams toward the shoulder/base units.

9. Sew a head unit to each body unit to complete four 6¹/₂" x 12¹/₂" Snowmen blocks.

10. Referring to Fusible Appliqué on page 92, prepare fusible appliqué pieces for the eyes and noses using the patterns given in the pull-out pattern section.

11. Fuse a nose and two eyes on each snowman head referring to the face pattern for placing the pieces. Stitch in place using black embroidery floss and a blanket stitch. Stitch five X's for a mouth on each snowman head.

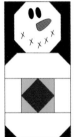
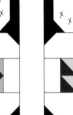

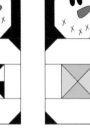

QUILT ASSEMBLY AND FINISHING

Note: Refer to the Assembly Diagram throughout the following steps. Press seams toward each border strip as added.

1. Sew a snowman block to two opposite sides of the Nine-Patch Star block to make the center row. Press seams toward the snowmen blocks.

2. Sew a Sawtooth Star block to the top and bottom of the remaining snowmen blocks to make the top and bottom rows. Press seams toward the snowman blocks.

3. Sew the center row lengthwise between the top and bottom rows to complete the 24¹/₂" x 24¹/₂" quilt center. Press seams open.

4. *Inner Border.* Sew the 1¹/₂" x 24¹/₂" gold print strips to two opposite sides and the 1¹/₂" x 26¹/₂" gold strip to the top and bottom of the quilt center.

5. *Outer Border.* Sew a 4¹/₂" x 26¹/₂" blue plaid strip to two opposite sides of the quilt center. Sew a 4¹/₂" red print square to each end of the two remaining 4¹/₂" x 26¹/₂" blue plaid strips. Press seams toward the strips. Sew these strips to the top and bottom of the quilt center to complete the top.

6. Layer, quilt and bind using the four 2¹/₂" x 42" green print strips, referring to Finishing Basics on page 93.

Assembly Diagram

Snowman Pillow & Wall Quilt

Make these accent projects by using the basic Snowman block from the table topper.
A few buttons or hand-stitched words add the final touch.

Skill Level: Beginner
Finished quilt/pillow size: 8" x 16"
Block size sewn into quilt/pillow: 4" x 12"
Number of blocks: 2

SUPPLIES
Yardage is based on 42"-wide cotton fabric.
- 2" x 3" piece black print
- 4" x 5" piece orange print
- 1/4 yard red/black/white plaid
- 1/4 yard cream/white print
- 1/4 yard green print
- 3/8 yard muslin
- 3/8 yard dark blue print
- 5/8 yard blue snowman print
- Two 10" x 18" pieces of batting
- Thread in colors to match fabrics
- 1/8 yard fusible web
- Five 1" buttons
- Black embroidery floss
- Embroidery needle
- Embroidery hoop
- Fiberfill stuffing
- Rotary cutter, ruler and mat
- Basic sewing supplies

CUTTING INSTRUCTIONS
From the black print and orange print, cut:
Appliqué pieces as per instructions

From the red/black/white plaid, cut:
Scarves as per instructions

From the cream/white print, cut:
One 4 1/2"x 42" strip; recut into two 4 1/2"
squares and two 4 1/2" x 8 1/2" rectangles

From the green print, cut:
Two 1 1/2" x 42" strips; recut into four 1 1/2"x
4 1/2" rectangles and four 1 1/2" x 14 1/2"
rectangles (border)

From the muslin, cut:
One 10" x 42" strip; recut into one 10" x 18"
rectangle (pillow lining)

From the dark blue print, cut:
One 1 1/2" x 42" strip; recut into sixteen 1 1/2"
squares
Three 2 1/2"x 42" strips (binding)

From the blue snowman print, cut:
Three 1 1/2" x 42" strips; recut into four 1 1/2" x
6 1/2" rectangles and four 1 1/2" x 16 1/2"
rectangles (border)
One 10" x 42" strip; recut into two 10" x 18"
rectangles (backings)

INSTRUCTIONS
Note: Use a 1/4" seam allowance throughout. Sew
all pieces with right sides together and edges
aligned. Press all seams to the darker fabric
when possible.

Snowman Blocks
1. Draw a diagonal line across the wrong side
of the 1 1/2" dark blue print squares.
2. Place a marked square right sides together
on each corner of the 4 1/2" cream/white print
squares and the 4 1/2" x 8 1/2" cream/white print
rectangles. Sew on the marked lines. Trim leaving a 1/4" seam allowance. Open and press toward
the dark blue corners to complete two head units
and two body units.

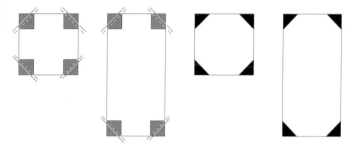

3. Sew a head unit to the body unit to complete
one 4 1/2" x 12 1/2" Snowman block. Press seam
toward the body unit. Repeat to make a second
block.

Make 2

4. Referring to Fusible Appliqué on page 92, prepare fusible appliqué pieces for the eyes and noses using the patterns given in the pull-out pattern section.

5. Fuse a nose and two eyes to each snowman head referring to the project photo for placing the pieces. Stitch in place using black embroidery floss and a blanket stitch. Stitch five X's for a mouth on each snowman head.

WALL QUILT ASSEMBLY AND FINISHING
Note: Refer to the Assembly Diagram throughout the following steps. Press seams toward each border strip as added.

Assembly Diagram 1

1. Sew a 1½" x 4½" green print rectangle to the top and bottom of one snowman block and a 1½" x 14½" green print rectangle to the long sides.

2. Sew a 1½" x 6½" blue snowman print rectangle to the top and bottom of the snowman block and a 1½" x 16½" blue snowman print rectangle to the long sides to complete the quilt top.

3. Layer the top with the 10" x 18" blue snowman print rectangle and 10" x 18" batting, quilt and bind using the three 2½" x 42" dark blue print strips, referring to Finishing Basics on page 93. Set aside remaining binding for pillow.

4. Tear two 1½" x 42" strips red/black/white plaid. Cut four 18½" long pieces. Lightly fray the edges. Set aside two pieces for the pillow. Tack two 18½" lengths at the snowman neck to make a scarf referring to the project photo.

5. Using black embroidery floss, sew the five 1" buttons down the center of the body unit to complete the wall quilt.

PILLOW ASSEMBLY AND FINISHING
Note: Refer to the Assembly Diagram throughout the following steps. Press seams toward each border strip as added.

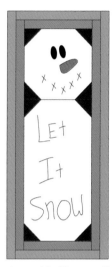

Assembly Diagram 2

1. Repeat steps 1 and 2 for the wall quilt to complete the pillow top.

2. Lightly trace the Let It Snow message onto the body unit.

3. Stitch the words using black embroidery floss and a stem stitch. (See Stitch Guide on page 92.)

4. Layer the pillow top with the 10" x 18" pieces of muslin and batting. Quilt as desired. Trim the backing and batting even with the pillow top.

5. Place the pillow top wrong sides together with the remaining 10" x 18" blue snowman print rectangle. Pin to hold together. Trim the rectangle even with the pillow top. Sew around the outer edge leaving a 6" opening on one long side.

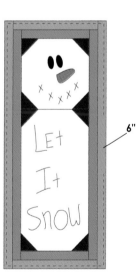

6. Stuff the pillow firmly. Stitch the opening closed.

7. Bind the edges of the pillow using the remaining dark blue print binding.

8. Tack the remaining 1½" x 18½" torn plaid strips in place on the snowman neck for a scarf to complete the pillow.

Chapter 9

The Noel Shoppe

Many years ago I often visited a favorite shop called The Noel Shop. This delightful Christmas shop was filled from top to bottom with all things Christmas. The owner was a very sweet woman who simply loved her customers and always had friends and family around when you visited the shop.

There are so many rooms in the Thimble Cottage Quilt Village, one simply had to be a Christmas room filled with all things Christmas and winter. Our Noel Shoppe is filled with a huge nostalgic Santa, Christmas trees decorated with all kinds of vintage ornaments, holiday table runners and Christmas tree skirts. The walls are covered with many types of quilts and the fireplace is topped off with three redwork quilted banners.

I love to do hand work. One of my favorite techniques is hand embroidery. The three redwork wall quilts in this chapter are easily stitched using red embroidery floss and simple embroidery stitches. I hope you make a few of these small quilts to decorate your home or to give as gifts. These projects are great take-and-go projects that can be stitched anywhere. Enjoy them all winter long.

Vintage Redwork Wall Quilts

Embroidery has been a very popular technique for centuries. Simple redwork embroidery is always a favorite. Enjoy a bit of bliss as you stitch these three wall quilts. To add a touch of sparkle, add crystals when the quilts are finished.

Skill Level: Beginner
Finished quit size: 13" x 19"
Number of quilts: 3

SUPPLIES

Yardage is based on 42"-wide cotton fabric.
- 5/8 yard cream/white print
- 1 yard red print
- Three 21" x 27" pieces of backing
- Three 21" x 27" pieces of batting
- Thread to match border
- Two skeins red embroidery floss
- Embroidery needle
- Embroidery hoop
- Fine-point pencil
- Clear crystals (optional)
- Rotary cutter, mat and ruler
- Basic sewing supplies

CUTTING INSTRUCTIONS

From the red print, cut:

Five 2 1/2" x 42" strips; recut into six 2 1/2" x 15 1/2" strips and six 2 1/2" x 13 1/2" strips (borders)

Five 2 1/2" x 42" strips (binding)

INSTRUCTIONS

Note: Use a 1/4" seam allowance throughout. Sew all pieces with right sides together and edges aligned. Press seams toward each border strip as added. Refer to the Assembly Diagrams throughout the following steps.

1. Prepare patterns for the Christmas Tree, Snowman and Santa Redwork Patterns given on the fold-out pattern page in the back of the book. Lightly trace the designs onto the 5/8 yard piece of cream/white print using the fine-point pencil. (Leave several inches between each design.)

2. Cut an 18" length of red embroidery floss. Separate into individual strands.

Leave space between designs

3. Thread the embroidery needle with one strand of floss. Place the embroidery hoop over one section of the design.

4. Stitch on the solid lines using a stem stitch, referring to the Stitch Guide on page 92. Stitch the Christmas tree garland with a chain stitch. Make a French knot at each solid dot on the designs.

5. Move the embroidery hoop to another section of the design as each section is completed.

6. When all stitching is finished, place a doubled towel on your ironing board. Place the stitched design face down on the towel and press from the back side.

7. Cut three 9 1/2" x 15 1/2" rectangles with a stitched design centered in each rectangle.

8. Sew a 2 1/2" x 15 1/2" red print strip to the long sides of each rectangle. Sew a 2 1/2" x 13 1/2" red print strip to the top and bottom of each rectangle to complete the quilt tops.

9. Layer, quilt and bind using the five 2 1/2" x 42" red print strips, referring to Finishing Basics on page 93.

10. Add a clear crystal to the center of each embroidered snowflake, if desired.

Assembly Diagrams

The Basics

In this section I've included general information about the embroidery stitches, fusible appliqué, and finishing techniques I use. Please refer to this section for information as you make the projects in this book.

STITCH GUIDE

Blanket Stitch

Stem Stitch

French Knot

FUSIBLE APPLIQUÉ

1. Purchase fusible web in the amount shown with each project. The projects call for 18"-wide webbing. If you use a narrower width, be sure to purchase extra.

2. All patterns in this book are already reversed for fusible appliqué, when applicable.

3. Trace the patterns on the paper side of the fusible web directly from the pull-out pattern page, or make a template for each piece and use the template to trace onto the paper side. If making a template, be sure to mark the side of the template that should face up when the piece is being traced.

4. Some of the patterns will need to be traced as is and also in reverse. For example, the Leaf pattern in the Daisy Days quilt is used in both ways. For any piece that must be reversed, make a template and

mark which side should face up to match the pattern in the pull-out pattern page. Trace with that side up and then flip the template over and trace it for the reversed pieces.

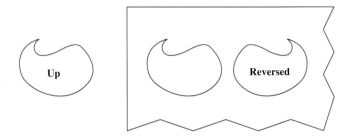

5. When tracing multiple pieces onto the web, leave about ¼"–½" between each piece. Roughly cut out the pieces leaving a margin around each one.

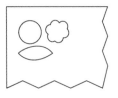

6. When several pieces will be prepared from the same fabric, trace them in a group on the webbing. Leave ¼"–½" around the group and trace the next pieces. Cut out the group as one unit.

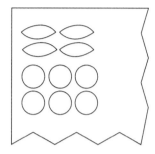

7. Fuse the webbing side of the pieces to the wrong side of the fabric referring to the manufacturer's instructions for iron temperature and length of time.

8. Cut out each piece directly on the traced lines.

9. Refer to the project photo to determine how the pieces will be placed on the background. Fold the background fabric in quarters or twice diagonally and finger-press to make creases to help align the pieces.

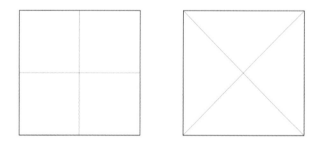

10. Remove the paper backing when you are ready to fuse the pieces to the background fabric.

11. Arrange the pieces on the background fabric referring to the project photo. When placed correctly, fuse in place.

12. Use a decorative or utility machine stitch around the outside of each fused piece to hold it in place. Use a matching or contrasting thread. Some of the projects use a blanket stitch. This may be done by hand or machine. For projects that will be laundered, be sure to use a stitch that completely covers the edges of the appliquéd pieces to prevent fraying.

13. If using a heavy decorative stitch, such as a very close satin stitch, cut a piece of fabric stabilizer. Place it behind the appliqué motif on the wrong side of the fabric. Pin it in place. Stitch around the edges. Remove the stabilizer when stitching is finished.

FINISHING BASICS

Layering, Basting and Quilting

All the projects in this book were machine quilted. You may choose to do your own quilting or take your projects to your machine quilter. Be sure that your batting and backing are at least 4" wider and 4" longer on each side of the project. The sizes you'll need are given in the Supplies section of each project. Here are the basic steps to do your own quilting.

1. Mark the quilt top with a quilting design, if desired. Place the backing right side down on a flat surface and place the batting on top. Center the quilt top right side up on top of the batting. Smooth all the layers. Thread-baste, pin, or spray-baste the layers together to hold while quilting.

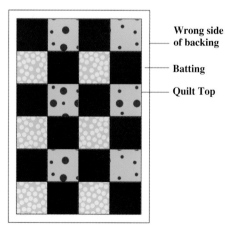

Wrong side of backing

Batting

Quilt Top

2. Quilt the layers by hand or machine. When you are finished quilting, trim the batting and backing even with the quilted top. If you will be adding prairie points to the edges of your project, do not trim.

Preparing Straight-grain Double-fold Binding

1. Cut strips as directed for the individual pattern. Remove selvage edges.

2. Place the ends of two binding strips right sides together at a right angle. Mark a line from the top left inside corner to the right bottom inside corner. Stitch on the marked line. Trim seam allowance to ¼".

3. Join all binding strips into one long strip. Press seams to one side. Fold the strip in half lengthwise with wrong sides together and press.

Preparing Double-fold Bias Binding

1. Place the 45-degree angle line of a rotary ruler on one edge of the binding fabric. Trim off one corner of the fabric.

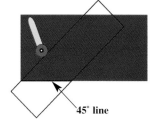

45° line

2. Cut binding strips in the width specified in the pattern from the angled end of the strip. Each strip cut from a ¼-yard piece will be approximately 12" long; each strip from a ½-yard piece will be approximately 25" long.

3. Cut strips to total the length needed for the pattern, repeating steps 1 and 2 as needed.

4. To join the bias strips, align the ends of two strips with right sides together. Stitch ¼" from the ends. Repeat to join all binding strips into one long strip. Press seams to one side. Fold the strip in half lengthwise with wrong sides together and press.

Sewing Binding to the Quilt

1. Leaving a 6"– 8" tail and beginning several inches from a corner, align the raw edges of the binding with the edge of the quilt. Stitch along the edge with a ¼" seam allowance, locking stitches at beginning.

2. Stop stitching ¼" from the first corner and lock stitching. Remove the quilt from your machine. Turn the quilt so the next edge is to your right. Fold the binding end up and then back down so the fold is aligned with the previous edge of the quilt and the binding is aligned with the edge to your right. Starting at the edge of the quilt, stitch the binding to the next corner.

3. Repeat steps to attach binding around the quilt, stopping stitching 6"– 8" from the starting point and locking stitches.

4. Unfold the two ends of the binding. Press flat. About halfway between the stitched ends, fold the beginning strip up at a right angle. Press. Fold the ending strip down at a right angle, with the folded edge butted against the fold of the beginning end. Press to crease folds.

5. Trim each end ¼" from creased fold. Place the trimmed ends right sides together. Pin to hold. Stitch ¼" from the ends. Press the seam allowance open.

6. Refold the strip in half. Press. Arrange the strip on the edge of the quilt and stitch in place to finish the binding.

7. Fold the edge of the binding over the raw edges to the back of the quilt. Hand stitch in place, covering the machine stitches and mitering the corners.

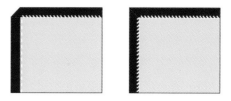

About the Author

I simply love to design projects that make people smile. Even as a child, I enjoyed making things from paper, clay, and fabric. I began my creative adventure as a child in 4-H. As a stay-at-home mother of three sons, I wanted to help with the household income, so over the years I developed many "Party Plan" marketing adventures by creating home-dec items.

I have been designing and creating projects for the creative industries for over 20 years. My first position was to design projects for a New York lace company. The projects were designed to increase sales of lace in the major chains. I also designed and set up the various booths for industry shows. I invented a needle called the Speedle during the time that I was designing for the lace company. The Speedle involved working with plastic infusion molding. I worked for the lace company for about 10 years.

I developed the Pearl Louise Designs pattern company in 1984. I have designed and produced more than 400 patterns for the quilt industry. I have written books for Plaid, Design Originals, Krause, and DRG/House of White Birches, and I self-published three more. I have designed and produced kits for Mary Maxim, Herrschners and House of White Birches. The McCall's Pattern Company also produces some of my designs. Many of my designs are included in various quilt magazines including *The Quilter*, *Fabric Trends*, *Quilt*, *Quick Quilts*, and *McCall's Quick Quilts*. I have designed gift lines for Seasons of Cannon Falls and Wang's International. Several years ago I started designing fabric for the Troy Corporation in Chicago. This has opened up many more creative doors, including two segments on public television.

I opened my quilt shop, The Thimble Cottage in 1995. I have six employees. We moved the shop into a larger space in 2006, at which time the name of the shop changed to the Thimble Cottage Quilt Village.

My husband, a CPA, has always been very supportive, and is an excellent guide when we fish for walleye. My hobbies include reading, embroidery, fishing, and my three darling grandchildren. One of my favorite sayings is, "Happiness is Homemade."

Every day is a new adventure.